102

D1120583

Fascinating Bible Topics

for

Group Discussions

A Spiritual Dictionary

User friendly for small groups, pastors, teachers and families.
Topics such as anger, comfort, fasting, forgiveness, justification, rewards.

Preston A. Taylor

PRESS

This book is dedicated to

Robert and Amy Marshall, a faithful couple in
Trinity Baptist Church of Mirando City, Texas. They use their time,
talents, and gifts for the glory of the Lord in their
local church and far beyond.

Additionally, this writing is a tribute to lay persons world-wide
who love Christ and His Kingdom cause and continue being
faithful to God, even though most will never be known
outside the area where they live.

FOREWORD

By
James Puckett, D. Min.

—ɯɯ—

When I was near the end of my studies at Southern Baptist Theological Seminary for my Doctor of Ministry Degree, it was just before Christmas. I had flown from San Antonio, Texas, where I was living to Louisville, Kentucky, to that potentially fatal and final meeting with my supervising committee composed of several professors. They had the power to approve my research or turn thumbs down bringing several years work to a disastrous end.

The commercial airport in Louisville was across town from the seminary. I called for a taxi for the nervous last ride, feeling like a condemned man in his last walk to the gallows. The taxi driver had several days stubble of beard and a foreign accent. As we drove toward the seminary, he asked me if I thought we should worship on Saturday or Sunday?

I groaned inwardly to think my final minutes were to be spent in this old argument. However, I was in for a pleasant surprise. My driver added that he thought the question was unimportant because we could worship God anywhere or anytime. Often, the back seat of his taxi had become a place of worship to his passengers for this was his place of ministry.

Things brightened up for me. As we arrived at the seminary, he got out of the taxi with me and asked to hold my hand while he prayed for me that God would be with me during my exam. I suddenly felt strangely strengthened by this simple, but profound new friend. I wondered if he were an angel sent to help me in my time of need. His encouragement sent me on to pass my examinations with flying colors. Thanks to my angel unawares!

Like my unexpected friend in the taxi, let me encourage you. I prayerfully recommend "102 Bible Topics...," a very valuable guide to every person who has the privilege of leading a group in Bible study. You have decided on God's Word, the greatest book in the world to study, and you have in your hand a superb guide written by Preston Taylor, an experienced and exciting author. You can be thankful you have discovered just the right direction to lead a Bible study.

Your great adventure has just become even more exciting with Preston's expertise to guide you. A thrilling time awaits you and your group members as you plow through these exciting topics. May God give you joy throughout this biblical journey!

Jim Puckett
Retired pastor,
First Baptist Church
McKinney, Texas

Chapter Titles

The Bible

Books of the Old Testament

The Pentateuch
Genesis…..Exodus…..Leviticus…..Numbers…..Deuteronomy

Historical books
Joshua…..Judges…..Ruth…..1 Samuel…..2 Samuel…..
1 Kings…..2 Kings
1 Chronicles…2 Chronicles…..Ezra…..Nehemiah…Esther

Poetical books
Job…..Psalms…..Proverbs…..Ecclesiastes…..Song of Solomon

Major prophets
(major because longer books)
Isaiah…..Jeremiah…..Lamentations…..Ezekiel…..Daniel

Minor prophets
Hosea…..Joel…..Amos…..Obadiah…..Jonah…..Micah…..
Nahum…..Habakkuk
Zephaniah…..Haggai…..Zechariah…..Malachi

Books of the New Testament

Biographical
Matthew…..Mark…..Luke…..John

Historical
The book of Acts

Paul's writing
Romans…..1 Corinthians…..2 Corinthians…..Galatians…..
Ephesians…..Philippians
Colossians…..1 Thessalonians…..2 Thessalonians…..
1 Timothy…..2 Timothy
Titus…..Philemon…..Hebrews (authorship debated)

General letters
James…..1 Peter…..2 Peter…..1 John…..2 John…..3 John…..Jude

Prophecy
Revelation

A Plan for Topical Bible Discussions in Small Groups

—ɯʋ—

This following is a topical Bible study approach for small groups. The purpose of this group study is manifold. Let's mention two benefits: First, each person should have joy in learning more about the Bible; also, the time in groups should enrich each one's life as you "search the Scriptures." Members of each group should have a Bible as well as a copy of this book to prepare for the discussion time. Some might wish (including this writer) that other topics had been included; however, there is a limit of the material that can be included in one project.

Remember that every Christian has difficulty finding some books of the Bible. Group leaders should remember that most everyone who comes to a discussion group wants to learn more about the Bible, even as we admit that no person knows everything about God's Word.

Who doesn't have a rather quizzical look when some Bible books are mentioned, such as Esther, Nahum, Habbakuk, Zechariah, or Jude? Be patient and help group members by indicating the general location of a Bible book.

In following this topical study, we go from "Genesis to Revelation." That is, the OT and NT references go in orderly progression.

The pastor or the one who directs all the groups should meet with group leaders and decide which topic is to be discussed in the next class period. Select the topic that seems most appropriate. The director of group leaders should review the topic with group leaders before the next sharing time with groups. Everyone should mark in his or her book the date and next topic for discussion. Group members should review the topic to be studied before the group meets each week.

In each group, allow time for each member to participate in reading the Scripture, praying, expressing herself or himself, etc. Ten Scripture references are generally listed in each unit; sometimes more than one session may be needed for a topic being discussed. The group should not rush through a topic that needs more time for discussion.

A word of caution is in order. Try to control the time for discussion, whether that is a 30 or a 45-minute study. Rarely ever should a leader take more than one hour with any study. Remember that you will meet again, therefore don't "wear out" the people, no matter how excited anyone may be about a topic. Try to give a balanced amount of time to each Scripture, knowing that some verses require more time than others.

This plan of group study lets each person become more familiar in handling God's Word. Everyone should have the opportunity to learn about the Bible, whether that one has been teaching for a half century, or whether the person has just begun to struggle with the matter of faith. Discussion time should be a school for learning, not a museum where one displays his or her wisdom.

You may order copies of the "102" by calling Xulon at their 24-7 book order line at 1-866-909-2665. (The "102" would be a great gift for a friend or some group that needs help). You may also order these books also by going to the website of XulonPress.com or ordering through Barnes and Noble or a religious bookstore. God bless you as you make the journey through these pages. As you begin each session, ask God to bless the time spent in His Word and fellowship with one another.

A-men

—〰—

We end our prayers with *a-men*. The word means *Let it be so.* The expression gives a strong approval of what has been said or done. In some churches years ago, a group of men would sit in a special area called the *a-men corner.* When the preacher said words they liked, they would say, *a-men.*

The Bible uses the word *a-men* more than seventy times. When people act in the way that God approves (both in the Bible context and in today's world), people often say *a-men.* When evil men hear a warning about the cost of doing wrong, the time for an *a-men* has come. When God provides good things for His people, we can say *a-men.* Frequently in the Scriptures, both men and women say *a-men.* Look at a limited selection of this remarkable word for this discussion time.

1. Deuteronomy 27:15. An a-men is given after a commandment that idol and image worshipers would suffer. What do you think about idolatry? What does God say?

2. Nehemiah 8:1-6. Where were the people when Ezra read from the *Book of the Law?* What did they do when he finished reading? What did the a-men mean?

3. Romans 9:4-5. What advantages did the Jewish nation have in the OT? Who came from that nation? Why should an a-men be said considering their advantages?

4. Romans 11:26-33. What does this Scripture teach us about God? Why does verse 36 teach about affirming God's blessings and His work?

5. Galatians 1:3-5. What has Christ done for us? What double blessings come our way because of Jesus? Why should one respond with an affirmation about these truths?

6. 2 Timothy 4:14-18. When Paul had no defenders, who came to His rescue? Who was the *lion* that wanted to kill Paul? Why did Paul say *a-men*?

7. Hebrews 13:20-21. Discuss these verses. What does the text say that God did for Christ? How does God act on our behalf? Why does this merit our *a-men*?

8. Revelation 1:5-7. What does Christ do for all who trust Him? What great event is in the future for God's people? How can we prepare for the future?

9. Revelation 5:14. What do you think of the *hymn of praise* to Jesus? Who sang it? What do you think of the a-men of this text?

10. Revelation 22:20-21. What does John say about Jesus? Why should an *a-men* be given at this place? Why should an *a-men* be sounded about God's grace?

Angels

—∿—

The word *angel* means *messenger*. Angels are supernatural beings who serve God and man. The Bible refers to angels about 200 times. Angels look like people when they become visible (Hebrews 13:2). The Sadducees of New Testament times did not believe that angels actually existed. Let's study a few references about them.

1. Psalm 34:7. What does the statement mean that angels surround God's people who fear Him? Do you think angels may surround us today? Why or why not?

2. Daniel 6:21-22. How did an angel help Daniel? Discuss the story. Do you believe that angels sometimes intervene in our lives today? How and why?

3. Matthew 4:11. After Christ fasted forty days, why do you think angels ministered to Him? What do you think they did for Jesus?

4. Luke 15:10. Do angels have interest in a person's salvation? How did the woman react when she found her money? What lessons does this parable teach?

5. Luke 16:22. Where was Lazarus, the poor man? What happened to him? Do you think it may be possible that angels have an ongoing ministry to dying believers?

6. John 20:12. How many angels sat in Christ's empty grave? What did one of them do? How did an angel illustrate the strength they have?

7. Acts 5:17-24. Who sent the apostles to prison in Jerusalem? Why? How did an angel help the apostles? What commandment did the apostles receive?

8. Hebrews 1:14. In what ways may angels possibly minister to God's people today? What did an angel do for Elijah. See 1 Kings 19:3-8.

9. Hebrews 12:22. How many angels did God create? What does this Scripture in Hebrews tell about the worship of angels?

10. Revelation 19:10; 22:8-10. What reaction did John have to an angel who appeared to him on the isle of Patmos? Should angels be worshiped? Why or why not?

Anger

—〰—

Most everyone becomes mad or upset at times. We usually attach a negative meaning to the experience of anger. However, anger also has its place in about anyone's life. Regardless of who we are, anger is one of the emotions that we continually face. Anger's range is as broad as life's experiences. Let's think about anger.

1. Genesis 4:3-7. Who were Adam and Eve's first two sons? Why did Cain become angry with his brother? What did he do? Why is anger potentially dangerous?

2. Exodus 4:14. Who was Moses? Why did God become angry with him? Can God become "upset" with people who should serve Him, but don't? Elaborate.

3. Numbers 22:27. Read all this chapter in Numbers. Who was Balaam? Why did he became angry? What kind of humor do you find in this unusual story?

4. 2 Kings 5:11. Who was Naaman? What reaction did he have to Elisha's message? How did Naaman's servant handle the situation? What would you do in such a crisis?

5. Proverbs 22:24. Is it wise to become a *bosom buddy* with a person who frequently becomes angry? Why or why not?

6. Jonah 4:1-7. How many times in chapter 4 is Jonah's anger mentioned? Why was he mad? Do you think that Jonah finally understood God's mission for him?

7. Micah 7:18. How does Micah describe God's actions? Do you believe that God becomes angry with those who don't repent? How can we help soften God's anger?

8. Mark 3:1-6. What did Jesus do that caused religious leaders to became upset with Him? What reaction did Jesus have to his critics? When is anger sometimes right?

9. Luke 15:28. In the Prodigal story, where was the older son and what did he do when the younger one left? Was the anger of the older brother right? Why not?

10. James 1:19. Why and when do we sometimes become angry too fast? Explain some ways that we can put *brakes* on the temptation of anger?

Baptism

—ᗯᗯ—

As an 11 year old child, I made my profession of faith during an evangelistic crusade. That night I tried to tell some more boys how my heart felt *spiritually warm*. The following Sunday afternoon our pastor baptized several of us in a lake in that community. The New Testament has several accounts of people who were baptized. We don't all agree on the details of baptism, but it is called a New Testament ordinance — whatever that word might mean to some! Let's look at some references.

1. Matthew 3:1-10. Describe John the Baptist. What did he demand of those who wanted to be baptized by him in the Jordan River?

2. Matthew 3:13-15. Who baptized Jesus? What two events took place when Christ was baptized? Why was He baptized? Who should be baptized? Why?

3. Matthew 28:19-20. What instructions did the disciples (apostles) hear from Jesus just before He ascended to heaven? What is involved in the *Great Commission*?

4. John 4:1-2. Why do you think that Jesus gained more disciples than John? Why do you think Jesus did not baptize His followers? What rumor circulated then?

5. Acts 2:38. What did Peter tell the Jewish converts to do? What gift would they receive? How far-reaching was the promise about the gift of the Holy Spirit?

6. Acts 8:26-39. Where was Philip when the Holy Spirit led him to meet a man from Ethiopia? What did Philip tell the man that he had to do before being baptized?

7. Acts 10:47. Who received the gift of the Holy Spirit as Peter preached? How did the Jews feel about the Gentiles? What did the Gentiles do when they believed?

8. Acts 22:6-16. What happened to Paul as he came near Damascus? Who was sent to help Paul when he arrived in Damascus? What did Ananias tell Paul to do?

9. 1 Corinthians 12:13. Paul wrote about a Spiritual baptism. Who baptizes believers into one body? What is that body? What does it mean to drink of one Spirit?

10. 1 Corinthians 15:29. The Bible *never* teaches *proxy baptism*. A Christian dies and the Holy Spirit convicts an unbeliever who says, *I believe and will take his place.*

Beatitudes or the state of utmost bliss

—⁓—

Children love to receive Christmas presents, birthday presents, and gifts at the end of school. Most of us would like to get our choice of presents any time, wouldn't we? Jesus talked about the gift or blessing of *utmost bliss* in his *Sermon on the Mount* in Matthew 5:1-12. What kind of blessings would you like for the Lord to give you today? Before beginning a discussion of the eight beatitudes, let's look briefly at the background of this study on beatitudes.

1. Matthew 3:1-4:25 What were some of the major events that took place in the life and ministry of Jesus immediately before the Sermon on the Mount?

2. Matthew 5:1-2. About how many people heard the Sermon on the Mount? Where was Jesus at that time? What did Jesus do as He started to teach? Why?

3. Matthew 5:3. Who are the *poor in spirit*? Are they proud and haughty? Are they spiritually empty and destitute? What does that mean? What is their reward?

4. Matthew 5:4. Do those who mourn refer to those who have sorrow over their spiritually bankrupt condition? How are they continually comforted?

5. Matthew 5:5. Who are the meek? Jesus expressed meekness as meaning submission to God, not weakness. What do the meek inherit? 1 Corinthians 3:21-22.

6. Matthew 5:6. What does it mean to hunger and thirst after righteousness? What does it mean *to be filled*? Why do some love backsliding more than right living?

7. Matthew 5:7. Who are the merciful? How can we show kindness and mercy toward those who are downcast or miserable? Why do we want God to be merciful to us?

8. Matthew 5:8. How can we be pure in heart? Is this a self-attained righteousness or is this an experience of being born again? What does it mean to see God?

9. Matthew 5:9. Do you think most people are in the peace-breakers or peace-makers camp? How can nations become peace-makers? What are peace-makers called?

10. Matthew 5:10-12. Name some Bible people who have been persecuted for the sake of righteousness. What of today? What are some rewards of the persecuted?

Birds

—ᴍᴍ—

The *Audubon Society* provides an amazing amount of informa-
tion about birds. Hundreds of species of birds live from the
jungles to the deserts. A few hymns or spiritual songs relate to birds,
such as *His eye is on the sparrow*. The Bible mentions more than
twenty different birds. We can learn fresh truths as we look at the
subject of birds.

1. Genesis 1:20-22. God made the birds and said they would
    multiply. Migratory and non-migratory birds cover this planet.
    Why are they God's gift to us?

2. Genesis 8:7; 1 Kings 17:6. After the flood, Noah sent out a
    raven and dove that flew back and forth until the water receded.
    How can birds serve as helpers to mankind?

3. Exodus 16:3. When the Israelites lived in the Sinai desert after
    leaving Egypt, God provided them quail to eat each evening.
    How did He do that?

4. Exodus 19:4. In an analogy, God said He carried His people
    from Egypt to the Holy Land on the *wings of eagles*. Why did
    many fall off on the journey?

5. Leviticus 5:7; Luke 2:22-24. Two pigeons were used for sin
    and burnt offerings. Two pigeons served at the consecration of
    Jesus. He identified with sinful man.

6. Proverbs 39:14. An ostrich lays her eggs on the sand. The feet of man or beast may destroy the eggs or the young of the careless ostrich. Apply this lesson to us.

7. Ecclesiastes 10:20. One expression states, *A little bird told me.* Why does this verse state not to whisper a bad word about anyone because a *bird* may take the message?

8. Ecclesiastes 12:4. Birds leave their roost early each day. During older years, many people get up at the *sound of birds.* Man's problems remain the same, don't they?

9. Matthew 3:16. When John baptized Jesus, God's Spirit descended upon Him like a dove — quiet and peaceful. What did God then speak from heaven?

10. Matthew 6:26; Luke 12:16. Birds don't plant crops nor gather them. However, God takes care of them. Does God remember us? Jesus asks, *Why worry?*

Blessed or blessings

—ᚲᚲ—

In the past century, Ira and Ann Yates traded their store for a wind-swept, cactus-infested ranch in Southwest Texas. A short time later, they signed a contract with an oil company to drill on their land. Amazingly, the first well produced 150,000 barrels of crude oil per day and other wells gave similar results. We would like to be blessed, wouldn't we?

The Bible tells about spiritual enrichment or blessings that go to those who walk in obedience to the Lord. Let's look at some of the blessings that can touch our lives.

1. Deuteronomy 15:7-11. What do we think or feel toward the poor? How will the Lord bless those who show kindness and generosity toward the *have-nots*?

2. Job 5:17. What does it mean to be corrected by the Lord? What advantages do we have for accepting God's discipline? How do you feel about God's discipline?

3. Psalm 32:1-2. What responsibility do we have when blessed by the Lord? What does it mean not to have sin counted against a person? Will God forgive all sin?

4. Psalm 112:1-2. What does it mean to fear the Lord? How can we delight in God's commands? How does God bless us when we reverence Him?

5. Proverbs 22:9. Do you know many generous people? Do people have to be wealthy to be generous? Why or why not? How does God bless the generous?

6. Isaiah 30:18. Do you struggle to wait on the Lord? Why? Why do we sometimes run ahead of God? How does God bless those who wait on Him?

7. Matthew 16:13. How did some recognize Jesus when He began His ministry? Who did Peter say Jesus was? Why did Peter's answer cause him to be blessed?

8. Ephesians 1:3-5. What is the source of spiritual blessings? Through whom do those blessings come? Why did God choose you and me?

9. James 1:12. How is a person blessed who endures trials? What are some tests that we face today? Tell about some blessings you have received when tested.

10. Revelation 1:3. What does it mean to hear God's Word? If we put into practice what God says in His Book, how will He bless us?

Blind or blindness

—⟋𝕨⟍—

Helen Keller became blind and deaf at the age of two. However, she graduated from Radcliffe College with honors and became a champion of the blind and deaf. One of the great handicaps that many people live with is blindness. To lack physical sight is an awesome problem. Many blind people have learned braille. Some blind people use white canes or have dogs to help them get around. And yet, the Helen Kellers of this world face difficulties that most of us never understand.

The Bible also mentions spiritual blindness. To suffer from the problem of not having spiritual sight is more critical than any of us fully realize. Let's look at the problem of physical and spiritual blindness from the biblical perspective.

1. Job 29:15. When Job's friends criticized him, he said that he was *eyes to the blind*. What did Job mean by that statement? How can we imitate Job?

2. Isaiah 59: 10. Isaiah described those without spiritual vision as those who grope for walls, stumble at mid-day, and act like dead men in desolate places. Is this so today?

3. Matthew 15:14. What did Jesus mean when He said that some leaders are like the blind who lead the blind? What happens to those leaders and to the ones they lead?

4. Matthew 23:24. Jesus faced critical religious leaders. What did He say about them and how do we interpret and apply His words about gnats and camels?

5. Mark 10:46-52. What kind of a crowd met Jesus in Jericho? As he left the city, who followed Him and asked for mercy? What did Jesus do? Can He help us now?

6. Acts 13:11. When Paul and Barnabas arrived on the island of Cyprus, they witnessed to Governor Sergius Paulus. Who opposed them? What did Paul do?

7. 2 Corinthians 3:14. Paul said the Israelites had a veil over their minds. What did he mean by that statement? How has Christ made it possible for the blind to see?

8. 2 Corinthians 4:4. Who blinds people to the truth of Jesus? What is the effect of people being blind to the gospel? Can you memorize this verse of Scripture?

9. Romans 11:25. What has happened in part to the Jewish nation? What advantage has this given to the Gentiles? When will *all Israel* be saved?

10. 1 John 2:11. If one believer hates a fellow Christian, where is he walking? Does he know where he is going? What action should he take so that he might see?

Blood

—🝫—

Mel Gibson produced *The Passion of Christ*, one of the best-viewed films of all time. Multiplied millions of people across the world sat in awe and shock as they witnessed the condemnation and beatings that Christ endured before His death on the cross. That sacrificial death that Christ made for mankind's redemption should always be the number one news story every where. Look at the references that relate to Christ's death and blood that He shed so that everyone might have salvation and life eternal.

1. Exodus 12:13. Before Israel left Egypt, they sprinkled blood upon the doors of their houses so the death angel would *pass over* them. What did that act prefigure?

2. Leviticus 17:11. The blood sprinkled upon the altar in the tabernacle indicated that Christ's blood would be shed for man's forgiveness. What else does this verse say?

3. Matthew 26:28. As Jesus instituted the *Lord's Supper*, what did the fruit of the vine symbolize? What is the benefit of those who believe in His blood?

4. Acts 20:28. What did Paul ask church leaders to do? How do leaders watch over fellow members? What does it mean that the church is purchased with His blood?

5. Romans 5:9. How do unsaved people become saved? What do the words mean about being justified by Christ's blood? How were Old Testament people justified?

6. Hebrews 9:14. Jesus offered His blood as a sacrifice that would cleanse the believer so that he or she could serve God. What kind of sacrifice did Christ make?

7. 1 Peter 1:18-19. What is not able to redeem or save a person? How is the blood of Christ described? Was there any blemish in the sacrifice that Christ made?

8. 1 John 1:7. What benefits do Christians have for walking in spiritual light? What will Christ's blood do for believers? What sins can be cleansed by Christ's blood?

9. Revelation 1:5. Christ is God's faithful witness who came alive after His crucifixion. What other title does He have? How are all believers cleansed from sin?

10. Revelation 7:14; 12:11. Any believer may go through *great tribulation*. How do they wash their garments and make them white? What are the steps to victory?

Boldness or bold

—✺—

A giant by the name of Goliath once stood before thousands of Israelite soldiers. That Philistine giant challenged any Israelite to fight him. All the Israelite or Hebrew soldiers shook with fear when the Philistine came before them. One day David appeared on the scene. He asked why everyone was afraid of Goliath. David rushed out to meet the enemy with five small stones, saying that he was coming to Goliath in the name of the Lord God of Israel. He hurled one stone at the giant, hitting him in the forehead, and the giant fell dead. What about our boldness for the Lord? Are we filled with courage, or does fear hold us in its grip? If we are bold for the Lord, we have freedom to speak in His name. Do you think most Christians are bold today? Look at what the Bible says about being bold in the Lord.

1. Proverbs 28:1. What do you know about lions? Who are the righteous? How do believers express their boldness? How can we be as bold as a lion?

2. Mark 15:43. What does this verse say about Joseph? Why did he go to Pilate? Do you think that act took courage on the part of the man from Arimathea? Why?

3. John 7:25-32. What did religious leaders want to do with Jesus? How did Jesus show that He was not afraid of them? How can we express Christ's boldness?

4. Acts 4:13. How did the crowd describe Peter and John? What special characteristic did the two apostles have? What gives God's people boldness?

5. Acts 4:31. When and where did this Scripture take place? What two great events happened in the "Upper Room" when believers prayed? How does praying help us?

6. Acts 9:29; 14:3; 19:8. Who did Paul confront with the message of Jesus? What did some want to do to him? How did Paul respond?

7. Ephesians 3:12. What's the source of one's spiritual boldness? Do you and I have confidence and freedom to talk to the Lord? Why or why not?

8. Ephesians 6:19-20. Why did Paul ask the saints of Ephesus to pray for him? Should we ask others to pray for us? Why did Paul want to be filled with boldness?

9. Hebrews 4:16. Do we have the authority and freedom to go into God's presence and speak with Him? Why or why not? What is the result of a bold approach?

10. 1 John 4:17. Do you think people need boldness as they face "the day of judgment?" Why? What helps us to become more bold and not be afraid of the future?

Cheer or encourage

—ᴍ—

Cheer leaders form a part of many sports events. This group has a big role to play for the spectators as well as for the teams. Churches need "cheer leaders." Pastors, teachers, ushers, and everyone else appreciate a "pat on the back" or a word of appreciation for what each one continues to do. Pastors should spend a lot of time encouraging their people rather than being negative. We are "God's ambassadors" of the best news the world has every heard. Therefore teachers, parents, pastors, and every Christian should be in the business of encouraging others. The Lord gives us an enormous amount of cheer along our pilgrim route too.

1. Deuteronomy 24:5. When young men married in Israel, they remained at home one year without military duty to cheer the wife. How can we cheer one another today?

2. Judges 9:13. Trees asked different plant life to rule over them. The vine said it's duty was to produce wine to "cheer 'the gods' and man." Does our job cheer others?

3. Proverbs 15:13; 17:22. Do you have a merry heart that animates your total life? How can one's attitude crush and dry up bones or produce good health like medicine?

4. Ecclesiastes 11:9-10. A warning is given about youthful pleasures that leave God out of life. What happens to anyone who lives for sinful indulgences?

5. Matthew 9:2. One day some men carried a paralytic to Jesus. He told the sick man to be cheerful because his sins had been forgiven. Discuss this story.

6. Matthew 14:27. In the midst of a storm, Jesus said to His disciples to be of good cheer. How could they have cheer? Will a boat sink when Jesus is present?

7. Matthew 16:33. What did Jesus tell the disciples they would face in the world? Has the situation changed? Why or why not? Why can we be cheerful today?

8. Acts 27:25, 36. Where was Paul at the time of the text? Who did Paul see and what message did he hear? How difficult is it for us to believe during harsh events?

9. Romans 12:8. What gifts do you have? How do you demonstrate them? What about the gift of encouragement? Can you show mercy with cheer? Who needs this?

10. 2 Corinthians 9:7. What's your attitude when an offering plate is passed? What is God's attitude toward a cheerful giver? Are you "hilariously happy" when you give?

Children

—⟋⟍—

Susanna Wesley, the mother of John and Charles Wesley, was asked how she was able to raise two sons as she did. She said, "By getting a firm grip on their hearts when they were young, and never turning them loose." Susanna and her pastor husband had nineteen children, and all walked in the steps of the Lord. When we think of rearing or raising children, most of us discover that hind sight is better than foresight. Even though we can't retrace life's steps, we can hold high the instructions that God has for children and youth, challenging them to go in God's ways.

1. Exodus 2:6-7. Refresh your minds on the beautiful story of the birth of Moses. What did the parents do for his welfare? What can we do to protect our children?

2. Psalm 127:3. Why are children an heritage from God? How are parents blessed when they have children? How can we help children be greater blessings?

3. Proverbs 4:1-27. This entire chapter presents the potential for rich blessings to be upon children. Select a few verses that speak to you about a good Rx for children.

4. Proverbs 20:11. What does it mean that a child is known by his or her actions? How are parents' lives reflected in their children? Why determines a child's behavior?

5. Proverbs 22:6. What does it mean to train a child? How much time should be given to children? How can we prepare children to go in the right direction?

6. Matthew 10:21. What causes some children to betray their parents? What does this mean? How can fathers help their children? Why do some children rebel?

7. Mark 10:13-16. What attitude did the disciples have about children? What response did Jesus make to their attitude? Discuss the treatment they received from Christ.

8. Luke 11:13. What often happens to children who are left without parents? What should a good father do for his children?

9. Acts 2:39. Simon Peter quoted from Joel 2:28-30 in his sermon at Pentecost. What promise did he say God would give to children as well as all believers?

10. Ephesians 6:1; Colossians 3:20. What promises are given to children who obey their parents? How does God feel about children who obey their parents?

Church

—⁓—

When people see a church building, the normal response is "That's the First Assembly of God church," "That's the First Methodist church," or "That's Pine Ridge Baptist church." We know that buildings do not compose a church; rather, the church is the people.

The Greek word for church is ecclesia which means "the called out ones." That is, those whose lives have been changed by the Holy Spirit and who gather to worship in Christ's name make up the body of Christ or the household of faith. Definitions vary, and we may quibble over church practices, but most of us would agree that the church is "the body of Christ," and He is the Head. Let's see a few references to the church from a few books or letters in the New Testament.

1. Matthew 16:13-20. Where were the apostles when Peter made his great confession? What did Jesus tell Peter? Who is the "rock" on which the church is built?

2. Acts 2:42-47. The fellowship of believers exploded with growth at Pentecost as the Holy Spirit filled their lives. Name a few of the actions of the church at that time.

3. Acts 8:1-4. Who led in the first persecution against the church? Has opposition to the church stopped? What should the persecuted believers do?

4. 1 Corinthians 3:11-17. Who is the foundation of the church? Why can't another foundation be laid? What or who constitutes God's holy temple?

5. 1 Corinthians 12:1-31. How is one enabled to say, "Jesus is Lord?" Who "baptizes" believers into one spiritual body (v. 12)? Why do members have different gifts?

6. Ephesians 1:22-23. What exclusive position does Christ have in His church? Where are "all things" in relation to Christ? What does this message mean to us?

7. Ephesians 2:14-22. What did Christ do about the position of the Jew and Gentile within the fellowship of believers? How does everyone have access to God?

8. Ephesians 4:11-12. Who are a few of the leaders within the church? Why do they have their positions? How do God's people build up the church and glorify God?

9. 1 Timothy 3:14-15. What instructions did Paul give the church in the first part of this chapter? How did Paul identify the church in verse 15? What does this mean?

10. 1 Peter 2:4-5. What does the expression about Christ being the "living stone" mean? Who are "living stones" and what "spiritual sacrifices" do we offer to God?

Comfort

—w—

When a baby begins to cry at 2:00 a.m., the child wants comfort. That one wants to eat or have some other attention from a parent. All of us "cry" for comfort or encouragement many times, don't we? The word "comfort" means to make comfortable, relieve pain, or solve some other problem. The Bible mentions comfort many times. Let's look.

1. Genesis 24:67. Isaac was the only son of Abraham and Sarah. Sarah died and Isaac was sad. Rebekah married Isaac and comforted him. Why do we need comfort?

2. Job 2:11; 16:1-5. How did Job's three friends show him comfort? What happened later with them and with Job? How did Job then react? How can we show comfort?

3. Psalm 94:19. When David felt anxiety-ridden, what did he do? Where did he find comfort? What did God's comfort do for David? How does God offer us help?

4. Isaiah 40:1-2. What commission did God give to Isaiah? How was Isaiah to speak to Israel? Why did he have a message of hope for them? How do we help others?

5. Isaiah 51:3. What good message did God have for Israel after their defeat and ruin? What would happen to their waste places? Why can God's people sing again?

6. Matthew 2:18. Who was Rachel and what happened to her children? What were the circumstances of that tragedy? Do sorrows still happen? What's our hope?

7. John 14:16, 26, 27. Why did the disciples of Jesus feel sad? What did Jesus promise to do for them? What does the "Comforter" do for believers? How can He help us?

8. Acts 9:31. How did the early Christians have the comfort of the Holy Spirit? What had they faced? How does the Holy Spirit strengthen and help us today?

9. Romans 15:4. How do the Scriptures give us comfort? How did the stories of the past teach the followers of Jesus? How do we find comfort today in God's Word?

10. 2 Corinthians 1:3-7. Why did Paul write that God is the God of all comfort? When does God comfort us? What should we do when we experience divine comfort?

Commandments — the 10

—m—

More than 600 laws were added to the Old Testament commandments to clarify or satisfy the whims of religious leaders. We probably could never count the number of laws that are on the statue books in any country to enforce people to "abide by the law." Ages ago God gave Moses the ten commandments. Jesus summarized those words by saying that we should love God and love one another. If we carried out these two commands most problems would be solved. Let's review the Ten Commandments which God has given.

1. Exodus 20:1-3. The first command gives emphasis to the Giver of laws. What did God do for His people? Why did He say not to have other gods before Him?

2. Exodus 20:4-6. What is an idol? Why didn't God want His people to worship idols? What happens to idol worshippers? What blessings go to those who love God?

3. Exodus 20:7. How does a person take God's name in vain or abuse His name? Why is one guilty who curses or uses God's name in vain? When are you guilty?

4. Exodus 20:8-11. What does is mean to keep God's day holy? Who should rest one day each week? Do you? What does it mean that God rested after creation?

5. Exodus 20:12. How does a person honor his or her mother and father? What promise is given to those who obey this command? How is this command violated today?

6. Exodus 20:13. Why is the command given not to murder? What is the difference between killing and murder? What about warfare? What about capital punishment?

7. Exodus 20:14. What is adultery? How did the Israelites disregard this command? What happens to family and community life when we disregard these words?

8. Exodus 20:15. Why is stealing so common? How does a person steal? Is each person entitled to his or her property rights? When does stealing take place?

9. Exodus 20:16. How does a person give false testimony against a neighbor? Where does this take place? How would you feel if someone told a lie about you?

10. Exodus 20:17. What does it mean to covet? Have you ever wanted property that belongs to your neighbor? What can coveting lead to? Did David covet?

Confession

—ɯ—

Sometimes when prisoners are taken captive during times of war, they may make true or false confessions because of punishment or other threats. Luke chapter 15 tells about a true confession of a prodigal who had wasted all his possessions in sinful living. He said that he would go home and tell his father the entire story of his life. He did exactly what he said he would do. His father welcomed him home, having a big celebration for him.

The word confession in Greek is homolego….That is, "I agree or confess by telling the truth." What would happen in the world and in churches if we had an honest time of true confessions? Look at a few references relating to the experience of confessions.

1. Proverbs 28:13. What happens to a person who hides his sins, rather than confessing them? What happens if we confess and forsake our wrong?

2. Daniel 9:4. Who did Daniel say had sinned? How had they sinned? How did they respond to the prophets? What was the result in the lives of those who failed?

3. Matthew 10:32. What does it mean to confess Jesus before others? How do we do that? What will Jesus do for those who confess and commit life to Him?

4. Romans 10:9-10. What does "confess Jesus with the mouth" mean? What does it mean to believe that God raised Jesus from the dead? What does it mean to be saved?

5. Philippians 2:11. Look at the previous few verses. How does a person confess that Jesus is Lord? What does that confession mean?

6. James 5:16. Should we be careful in confessing faults to one another? Is it always easy to pray for one against whom we may have sinned? Does prayer have effect?

7. Hebrews 11:13-16. Why do we have a strong love for this world? Is it hard to think of ourselves as strangers and pilgrims in the world? Why or why not?

8. 1 John 1:9. Do you find it easy to confess your sins? Why should our sins be confessed? To whom do we admit our sins? What happens when we confess?

9. 1 John 4:15. Do you believe that Jesus is the son of God? Why do you believe this? What takes place within a believer who confesses that Christ is God's son?

10. 2 John 1:7. Many false prophets and so-called religious people say that Jesus is not God's son? What two descriptions are given to such people?

Cross of Christ

—ɯ—

Arthur Blessitt grew up in Mississippi. For more than thirty years he carried a heavy cross on almost every continent. He's walked through thirty or forty countries, sharing the message of Jesus face to face with countless people. Also, he has spoken on television programs dozens of times. Look at what the Bible states about the cross.

1. Matthew 16:24. What three requirements did Jesus give for those who want to be His disciples? Have we minimized these conditions for being Christ's followers?

2. Matthew 27:40-42. How did religious leaders ridicule Jesus as He was dying on the cross? Do you think if Christ had come down that they would have trusted Him?

3. 1 Corinthians 1:17. What did Christ call Paul to do? Did he speak against baptism? How can the cross be emptied of its power?

4. Galatians 6:14. What was Paul's source for boasting? What did the cross mean for him? What does it mean to be crucified to the world? How does this effect us?

5. Ephesians 2:16. How does being reconciled or brought back to God take place? What happens to the hostility that existed between man and God?

6.   Philippians 2:6-9. What did Jesus become when He came to the earth? How can a person describe the suffering of Christ on the cross? Where is Jesus now?

7.   Philippians 3:18. Paul stated that many were enemies of the cross of Christ. What does that mean? How is the hatred of the cross expressed?

8.   Colossians 1:20. How are all things in heaven and on earth reconciled to God? What does the blood that has been shed on the cross provide for the believer?

9.   Colossians 2:14-15. What two great transactions took place through the cross? What did Christ do with the Old Testament laws and ordinances that were against us?

10.   Hebrews 12:2. What did Jesus expect beyond the cross? What cost was involved in Christ's death on the cross? Where is He now? Does Jesus die anymore?

Death — physical and spiritual

—w—

Physical death is a common experience. Thousands of people die every day across the world as a result of illness, accidents, wars, starvation, and the list goes on. Cemeteries all over this planet testify to the fact that death is a reality. Some die because of abortion, some while young, some in the middle years of life, and some when they become "old and feeble." Let's see some things which the Bible says about death.

1. Genesis 2:15-17. What did God tell Adam would happen to him if he ate of the forbidden fruit? What two deaths did Adam suffer? Will we die? When?

2. 2 Kings 20:1-7. What did Isaiah tell King Hezekiah? What does it mean to "set one's house in order?" How do we do that? How can we extend life?

3. Psalm 23:4. Why is death called "the shadow of death?" Who is with us when the time of death comes? What should be our reaction as we face death?

4. Psalm 90:9-10. How do many people pass their years? What is the normal life span? Why do we need wisdom? Who gives us wisdom so that we can live right?

5. Psalm 116:15. How does God evaluate the "home going" of His people? Why? How does a statement about death being "precious" prepare you for the event?

6. Isaiah 57:1-2. What is a big advantage for the believer when that one leaves this life? What condition of life do the righteous have when they die?

7. 1 Corinthians 15:54-58. What question is given to death in these verses? How is death's sting removed? What is our victory? What should we do before we die?

8. 2 Corinthians 5:1-5. What kind of body will God give us when we die? What is our guarantee of a better life after death?

9. Philippians 1:21-23. What struggles do God's people often face before death? Why is it often profitable for others if we don't die now? What's the advantage if we die?

10. Revelation 1:18. What did Jesus mean when He said that He *was* dead, but now is alive forever more? What does it mean that Christ has the keys of death?

Discern or discernment

—m—

The book of Genesis gives the story of Jacob's visit with Isaac, his father. Jacob and his mother made a plan so that Isaac would give family blessings to Jacob, rather than to his older twin brother, Esau. When Jacob told Isaac that he had come for his blessings, Isaac felt of Jacob's arms that had been covered with goat hair and he said, "Your voice is the voice of Jacob, but you feel and smell like Esau." He was not able to discern the difference, and gave his blessings to Jacob. The Bible challenges us to be able to tell the difference between the true and false, between the inferior and superior.

1. 1 Kings 3:9. When Solomon became king, he asked God to give him a "discerning heart" to govern Israel. How does discernment help with family, work, etc?

2. Proverbs 7:6-27. A "guy meets a gal." She is a prostitute who traps him. He is like an ox going to slaughter. What is the difference between love and lust?

3. Proverbs 10:4; 13:4. Do people know the difference between diligent hands and those of a sluggard? What happens to both kinds? Which is preferable? Why?

4. Ecclesiastes 8:5. From the "wisdom book," a need is indicated for discernment about the right time and right procedure for every matter. How does this idea apply to us?

5. Ezekiel 44:23. Israel's priests had the job of teaching how to know the difference between the secular and the sacred, the clean and unclean. Is this lesson for now?

6. Malachi 3:18. God says when He "gathers his jewels," He will know those who serve Him and those who don't. How do we get ready for His evaluation?

7. Luke 12:56 (Matthew 16:2-3). Jesus told a few religious leaders that they could "discern the sky," but not the present time. What did Jesus mean by His words?

8. 1 Corinthians 2:14 (1 Cor. 12:10). Without the Spirit of God, is man able to discern the things of God? Is he able to "discern the spirits?" Why or why not?

9. Hebrews 5:14. Spiritual food such as Bible study, prayer, and fasting help us to see the difference between good and evil. What are some examples of both?

10. 2 Peter 3:10-14. Since the final "day of the Lord" will end the world system, why should God's people be careful about the way they live? How should we live?

Evangelism or witnessing

—∿—

Larry Gross spent seventeen years in and out of jails in Pennsylvania. One day while out of jail, Larry read a gospel tract that someone had left on a park bench. Soon thereafter, the Lord saved that struggling, wayward Jew. Since that time, Larry has become the "Cross Man," taking a heavy cross up and down highways across Texas and beyond.

People by the hundreds have stopped on the highways to talk to Larry. He has spoken to thousands and has given out tens of thousands of gospel tracts. Some wonder how they may witness for Christ. In what ever way God's Spirit leads, we can be a testimony for Christ. A few Scriptures challenge us to witness.

1. 2 Kings 7:39. Where were four leprous men and what was their decision? What did they do when they discovered that Israel's enemies had gone? Apply the story.

2. Psalm 126:5-6. The scene is agricultural. What "seed" do we have to share? How are we to "go forth?" How can we often return from a witnessing venture?

3. Proverbs 11:30. Why is a person wise who wins others to Christ? Do the converts find a better life? Is the one who witnesses blessed? Does the devil lose anything?

4. Isaiah 6:8, 11-12. What response did Isaiah have to the Lord's call to witness? How long did God tell him that he should witness? Are we ready to respond? Why?

5. Jeremiah 20:9. Did Jeremiah become tired of witnessing? What happened to him when he said that he would stop? What about the "fire" within us?

6. Daniel 12:3. What does the sky look like on a clear night? Do many stars shine? What happens to people who turn others to righteousness? Are you now glowing?

7. Matthew 28:18-20. What is the resource for witnessing? What is the commission for every Christian? Where do we start? How far are we to reach? Are we doing it?

8. Luke 24:45-49. What was the occasion of this passage? What did the apostles do when Jesus ascended? What story did they have to tell? What's our message?

9. Acts 1:8. What did the apostles need to be effective in Christ's cause? Are Christians effective in telling about Jesus today? Why or why not? What can we do about it?

10. Acts 26:22-23. What did Paul say about his help? Who heard his testimony? What was his message? What is our message? Are we telling the Story? Why or why not?

Faith

—◊—

Some of God's great people across the centuries have doubted Him. When Moses led the Israelites from Egypt across the Red Sea into the big wilderness area south of the "Holy Land," they complained to Moses. They said that in Egypt they had flesh to eat, but they were going to starve to death where they were.

Moses talked to God about the problem. God told Moses that He would give the people flesh to eat not just for one or two days, not for five, 10, or 20 days, but for an entire month. He said He would give them meat until it started coming out of their noses. Moses told the Lord that the Israelite men numbered 600,000 and that to feed them and their families meat for one month would require killing all their cattle and eating all the fish in the oceans! God said, "Just wait, Moses!" That night God sent a wind that brought so many birds into their camp that they could not begin to kill and eat them all. What about your faith? Let's see what the Bible says about faith.

1. 2 Chronicles 20:20. If we have faith in God, what will happen? What does it mean to be established? If we believe the message of God's Word, what happens? Why?

2. Habakkuk 2:4. How can a person deceive himself or herself? What does it mean to have the soul lifted up? How do people who are just live? What does this mean?

3. Matthew 17:20. What did Jesus mean when he said a person with faith could be a "mover of mountains?" How and why does faith make miracles possible?

4. Luke 17:5. What did the disciples ask Jesus to do for them? How does Christ increase our faith? In what areas of life do you need more faith today?

5. John 6:28-29. The apostles asked Jesus what they should do in order to do God's works. What did Jesus say to them? What does it mean to believe on Jesus?

6. Romans 5:1. Why should every person memorize this verse? How does faith justify the believer? What is the benefit of being justified or being made right with God?

7. Ephesians 6:16. How important is a shield in battles, such as armor-plated vehicles? How does the shield of faith protect a person? Name a few "fiery darts" we face.

8. Hebrews 11:6. Why is it impossible to please God without faith? What does it mean to believe God as we come to Him? How does God reward those who seek Him?

9. James 2:17. How does real faith express itself? If a person's so-called faith does not respond to needs that can be at least partially met, what about that kind of faith?

10. 1 John 5:14. What is necessary for a person to find victory over the world? What constitutes victory over the world? What are some of the world's allurements?

Fasting

—ᴡ—

Most everyone eats breakfast. After a long or short night without food, some feel half-starved. The word "breakfast" means "break the fast." In Spanish, "desayuno" means breakfast. The Spanish word "des" has the idea of stopping the "ayuno" or fast. Thus, in Spanish or English we stop the fast when we begin to eat. Even though we don't hear much about this ancient biblical habit, we should give attention to it.

1. Deuteronomy 9:9, 18-21. Moses walked to the top of a mountain and received the commandments. He fasted for a long time because of Israel's sins. Should we fast?

2. 2 Samuel 12:15-23. David fasted while his first child lived. When the baby died, he ended his fast and returned to his normal duties. Discuss the story.

3. 2 Chronicles 20:1-30. When Israel faced enemies, King Jehosaphat called for a fast. God told him that the battle was His, not to fear. Discuss and apply the story.

4. Ezra 8:21-23. When Ezra prepared to leave Babylon after the captivity, what did he and the Hebrews do? What did they ask of God? What did God do for them?

5. Isaiah 58:1-14. During the fast of some Hebrews, they "fussed, fumed, and fought." What did God tell them to do. The lessons are essential. Discuss them.

6. Jonah 3:5-10. About 120,000 people in Nineveh heard Jonah preach for 40 days. What did everyone do? What did God do? How does this story apply to us?

7. Matthew 6:16. Why was Jesus critical of the fasting habits of many religious leaders? How does God feel about those who openly display their religion?

8. Luke 2:37. Anna was an 87 year old widow who was a prophetess. What had she been doing since her husband's death years earlier? What message did she give?

9. Luke 18:12. A Jew who collected taxes from his nation for the Roman government found acceptance with God. What problem did the religious Pharisee have?

10. Acts 13:1-3. The church in Antioch fasted and prayed. What message did the Holy Spirit give them? What happened next? What do you think about fasting?

Feet

—〰—

Most of us have two feet. A small percentage of people suffer a critical handicap of not having one or both feet. Birth defects, injuries, or illnesses may rob a person of his or her feet. Some people have big feet, wearing a size 14 shoe. Most ladies have smaller feet. We buy new shoes for children every year because their feet grow so fast! The Bible mentions mankind's feet many times. Think about them.

1. Genesis 18:4. Abraham washed the feet of angels, not knowing who they were. Why did he do that for his visitors? Are we ready to wash the feet of others?

2. Joshua 10:24. Joshua told some Israelites one day to put their feet upon the necks of five pagan kings? Why did he give that command? What did that mean?

3. 2 Samuel 9:13. Who was Mephibosheth? What happened to him? How did David help him? How do we help unfortunate people? Can you help someone today?

4. Psalm 119:105. What could happen to a person who walks or drives without lights at night? How can we help others in a world that is dark and sinful?

5. Proverbs 4:14, 15. In which directions can feet take us? What path is the best one to follow? How can we avoid an evil path? Do right choices come automatically?

6. Isaiah 52:7. When you get home today, take a new look at your feet. Are they pretty? How can feet be made beautiful? Are you ready for this transformation?

7. Lucas 1:79. Who has come to guide our steps? In what one area does Christ want to direct our feet? Do most people want to live in peace? Why or why not?

8. John 13:5. Tell the story of Jesus and His disciples in the Upper Room? What did Jesus do? What did His disciples learn from that experience? What about us?

9. Acts 16:24. What happened to Paul and Silas in this story? Did they suffer? What reaction did they have? How do we respond to trials?

10. Revelation 1:17. Where was John and who did he see? What did the apostle do when he saw Jesus? What attitude should we have in Christ's presence?

Fools

—⚬—

In centuries gone by, kings and other royalty had what was then called "court jesters." The jesters often wore "dunce caps" and tried to entertain their guests with outlandish remarks and acts. Often times, they were referred to as fools.

A fool is a person who lacks wisdom by frittering life away on non-essentials. They spend time thinking and doing the frivolous, with little thought of important issues for themselves, their families, and others.

The Bible refers to fools several times, cautioning people not to live that kind of life. We will look at several verses from the Old and New Testaments that give insight into the life of a foolish or wasteful person.

1. Psalm 14:1; 53:1. These two Psalms are practically identical. Even with the evidence of creation, the Scriptures, Jesus, and history, the fool denies God. Why (14:3)?

2. Psalm 107:17. What causes a person to become a fool? What are the results? What afflictions do foolish people suffer?

3. Proverbs 10:8, 10, 21, 23. What happens to a chattering fool? What brings about their death? Where do they find pleasure?

4. Proverbs 12:15, 16; 13:16; 14:1. What do fools think about their own way of life? What reactions do they sometimes express? What do they do with their folly?

5. Proverbs 14:7-9. What action can a foolish woman take? What does that mean? Comment on the mouth, lips, and tongue of a fool.

6. Proverbs 18:6-7; 24:7. What does a fool's words cost him? Is this serious? What kind of association does a fool miss? What does this mean?

7. Jeremiah 4:22. Describe some of the ways that God's people lived. Were they foolish? Is that "old way of life" practiced today? When and why?

8. Ecclesiastes 2:14; 10:15. What does it mean to walk in darkness? Do many people miss the right way? How do fools feel about work? What's your reaction to duty?

9. Luke 12:16-20. What is God's declaration of a person who has no time or room for Him? What's the result? Why do people try to get along without God?

10. 1 Corinthians 4:10. What does it mean to be a "fool for Christ's sake?" How can we imitate Paul's way of life? Are we involved in being a new kind of fool for Jesus?

Forgetting

—∿—

Ex-President Ronald Reagan suffered from Alzheimer's disease during the last years of his life. This kind of illness strikes the central nervous system, causing its victims to have a premature mental degeneration. We may be healthier if some memories can be forgotten. However, we should not overlook and forget life's blessings. Some people suffer from "intentional alzheimers," trying to escape responsibilities. Let's consider this eclectic topic of forgetting.

1. Genesis 40:23. What did Joseph do for Pharaoh's cup bearer? What favor did Joseph ask of him? What did the cup bearer do? Why do we forget those who help us?

2. Deuteronomy 4:23-24; 6:10-12. What did Moses tell the Israelites to do when they settled in the holy land? What warning did he give them? What is the application?

3. Job 19:14. The Bible calls Job a godly man who helped others. When troubles came to Job, what did his friends and kinsmen do? What does this story teach us?

4. Psalm 9:17. What happens to the wicked when they die? What else? What happens to nations that forget God? What dangers do nations face today?

5. Jeremiah 3:32. What reaction would people have at a wedding, if the bride came to the wedding without her wedding dress and jewelry? Why do we forget God?

6. Jeremiah 23:33-39. What kind of message do false prophets have? How can God's message or Word be distorted? What happens to false teachers?

7. Philippians 3:13. What are some matters in life that we should forget and not hold to? Why? Is it always easy to forget what needs to be forgotten?

8. Hebrews 10:17 (Psalm 103:12; Micah 7:19). What does God do with our sin that is confessed and forgiven? For how much time does God forget our sins?

9. Hebrews 13:2-3. What groups of people should not be forgotten? Where are these people located? What can we do to minister to them? Are you ready to help?

10. 2 Peter 1:9. What are a few practical issues of the Christian life that Peter mentions? What happens if we forget the basics? How does forgetting hurt us?

Forgiveness

Someone asked a young black girl from an island in the Carribbean what she had learned since becoming a Christian. She answered, "I have learned to forgive the man who killed my father." Forgiveness is not always easy. It costs to forgive. However, God's way is for us to learn how to forgive. Look at some Scriptures on forgiveness.

1. Nehemiah 9:16-17. Nehemiah confessed that their ancestors had been arrogant and disobedient. Then he stated, "But you forgive." Do we know that God forgives?

2. Isaiah 55:7. Why should people seek the Lord? What sins do we commit? If we turn to the Lord, what will He do? To what degree will God forgive?

3. Matthew 6:14-15. When we forgive someone who sins against us, what will God do? What if we refuse to pardon anyone who offends us? Are you ready to forgive?

4. Matthew 18:21-22. Simon Peter seemed to be a "stickler for the law." He asked if forgiveness needed to be more than seven times. What did Jesus say?

5. Luke 17:3-4. Have you ever read these verses before? Has anyone ever offended you seven times in a day, asking forgiveness each time? What's the normal reaction?

6. Luke 23:32-34. What did some people say to Jesus while He was dying on the cross? What did Jesus say? Why did He say those words? Do we sin in ignorance?

7. Acts 13:38. What good news may be announced through Jesus to a sinful world? Where do some people look for pardon? Is Jesus the only way to have salvation?

8. Ephesians 1:7. What does it mean to be forgiven through the blood of Jesus. How rich is God's grace? What can we say to friends who need God's forgiveness?

9. Colossians 3:13. Do we need to put up with the grievances that come our way from others? How are we to forgive?

10. 1 John 1:9. If we want forgiveness, what must we do? What does "confess" mean? When we confess our sins, what does God do? Does forgiveness cover all sin?

Fruit or fruitful

—〰—

Most people eat fruit. What's your favorite? Let's play a game. Let's name as many fruit as we can think of. The Bible mentions fruit many times. Let's think for a little while about fruit and the fruitful life.

1. Genesis 1:11-12. God placed plants and trees on this earth. What is necessary for fruit trees to produce good fruit? What is necessary for us to be fruitful?

2. Numbers 13:26. God wanted Israel to leave their desert life and go into Canaan. What did the spies see in that place? Why did they miss their blessings?

3. Psalm 92:12-14. How can the righteous flourish like a palm tree? Can God's people bear fruit in later years? How do they live and what can they say or proclaim?

4. Matthew 7:15-20. False prophets are known by their fruit. What happens to those who do not produce good fruit? What is the message of verses 21-23?

5. Luke 13:6-7. A man cultivated fig trees for three years, but the trees had no fruit. What did the owner say? What did the worker say? How does this apply to us?

6. John 15:2. What does Jesus do with His people? Why does He "prune" us? What thoughts and activities need to be cut away from our lives? How do we do it?

7. John 15:16. How does Christ choose His people? Why? When do we know if our fruit is "lasting?" How does God bless those who are fruitful?

8. Romans 7:4. How do we die to the old life? (Galatians 2:20). If we die, do we come to life in the Spirit? What are two results of the resurrected life in Christ?

9. Galatians 5:22-23. Do most Christians become fruitful? Who makes possible the fruitful life? Discuss the fruit of the Spirit that this text mentions.

10. Colossians 1:10. Why should we pray for one another? What does it mean to "bear fruit in every good work?" What are some good works where we should be fruitful?

Friends

—⁂—

A town or city in Texas has the name of Friendswood. That growing city south of Houston began with a religious group called "Quakers" or "Friends." A friendship circle with true friends is a blessing to one person or to many people. The Bible reminds us of friendship links. Consider this topic for discussion.

1. 1 Samuel 18:1-4. Who was Jonathan? When did his friendship with David begin and how long did it last? Where can we meet friends?

2. Job 2:11-13. What were the names of Job's first three friends? Why did their friendship "cool off?" What happens when we begin to criticize friends?

3. Psalm 41:9. Who was the "false friend" of Jesus, and what did he do? (See Matthew 26:14, 47-50). How do we betray Jesus?

4. Proverbs 17:17 State some ways that friendship expresses itself. Do friends always agree? Does Proverbs 18:24 tell how to have friends? Who is the best friend?

5. Zechariah 13:6. What were the "wounds" in Christ's body. Who were those in the house of Christ's friends? Can we cause wounds in God's kingdom today?

6. Matthew 11:19. Did Jesus include some unusual people in His friendship circle? Should we be friends of some on the "outside?" Why or why not?

7. John 11:35-36. What did Jesus do when He stood near the grave of Lazarus? Why? How do we encourage and support others at a difficult time in their lives?

8. John 15:13-14. What did Jesus call His followers? How do Christ's friends prove their friendship? Do you have friends who need to become friends of Jesus?

9. James 2:23. Why was Abraham called "the friend of God?" What great sacrifice was Abraham ready to make for God? (See Genesis 22:1-14). What about us?

10. 3 John 1:14. Can you call the names of a few friends? Why do we need friends? How can we improve our friendship with others?

Glory or glorious

—∿—

Franz Haydn (1732-1809) produced his musical work called "The Creation" in 1798. One year before his death, his friends took Haydn to hear the performance of that masterpiece in his home city of Vienna, Austria. As the orchestra and choir played and sang, they came to the words, "And there was light." The crowd stood in applause. Hayden stood and with trembling hands, pointed heavenward saying, "No, no, not from me — from heaven above comes all!"

How blessed of God our nation and world would be if we would give glory and honor to the Lord in all things! More than 500 times in the Bible the words "glory, glorious, and glorified" appear. Let's consider a few Scriptures that refer to God's glory.

1. Exodus 33:18-23. What request did Moses make of God? Where did God place Moses before he saw the Lord's glory? Should we make that request today?

2. 1 Samuel 4:12-22. What tragic news did the wife of Phinehas hear? What did she name her son? Why? Why does God's glory depart from a nation or church?

3. 1 Chronicles 29:10-13. Discuss the praise that David gave to God. What word did he use to describe God's name? Why is the divine name glorious?

4. Psalm 24:7-10. When does the King of glory fill our lives? Who is the King of glory? How can we give the King of glory total control of life?

5. Psalm 145:10-13. Who and what should praise and glorify God? Why should we tell of the glory of our King? How do we share this message of the Lord of glory?

6. Haggai 2:6-7. Who is the "Desire of all nations?" What promise did God give about the rebuilt temple? Who composes God's temple? How can He fill us with glory?

7. Luke 9:28-33. As Christ prayed, what happened to Him? What kind of appearance did Moses and Elijah have? What does this tell us of our future life?

8. Romans 8:21. What will happen to creation one day? Who will change creation from decay to a glory-filled life? Why should God's future work cause us to glorify Him?

9. 1 Corinthians 10:31-32. Have you thought about glorifying God with your life-sustaining habits? Why did Paul say he tried to glorify the Lord? What of us?

10. 2 Corinthians 3:7-11. The ministry of the Law on stone came with God's glory. Why is the glory that lasts greater than the "Old Covenant" glory?

Go or traveling

—∭—

If you have been to an airport lately, you know that such places are filled with planes and people. Take a look at any highway, night or day. Eighteen wheelers and vans and cars — they never seem to stop. We are on the go always. One fellow who became tired of traveling said, "My get up and go has got up and went." What about our going for the Lord? What about the devil who is always on the go? Let's see how the little word "go" can fit into a Bible lesson.

1. Job 1:7. The Lord asked Satan one day, "Where have you been?" He answered, "From going to and fro upon the earth?" What's the devil doing now?

2. Psalm 58:3. Innocent-appearing children get into mischief fast. The Psalmist says they get into trouble as soon as they're born. Share some experiences you've had.

3. Proverbs 26:20. Have you ever started a fire with wood? What happens if all the wood is burned? What's the best way to stop a quarrel, rumor, or gossip?

4. Matthew 5:4. Roman soldiers sometimes ordered Jews to carry their packs for a mile. How could a friend be made of the soldier? How can we go the second mile?

5. Matthew 28:18-20. Where did Jesus say His people are to go? Where does that journey start? What do we do as we go? How long does Jesus stay with us?

6. John 6:67-68. A big crowd came into a desert area. After they had eaten, what did they do? What did Jesus ask His disciples? Where can we go if we leave the Lord?

7. John 8:1-11. Who did a few religious leaders "corner" in the temple? What did they ask Jesus? What was Christ's message to them? What did Jesus say to the woman?

8. John 14:1-2. Where did Jesus say that He was going? Why was He going to leave them? What did Jesus tell them He would do? How can we go to be with Christ?

9. Ephesians 4:26-27. Is it evil to become angry? Did Jesus ever get mad? What's the "dead line" for anger? Who takes advantage of the one who stays mad? How?

10. Hebrews 6:1. What does it mean to "go on to perfection?" Are we ever sinless? How do we become mature? Should we all keep growing? Who is our model?

God

—∿—

An old anecdote illustrates a great truth. Someone watched a boy drawing a picture. When the question was asked what he was doing, he answered, "I am drawing a picture of God." He then was told that no one knows what God looks like and that he could not draw God's picture. He said, "When I get through with this picture, everyone will know what God looks like."

The truth is that we can never fully know God. He's always "beyond us." However, the Bible has hundreds of Scriptures which give insight into what God is like. We will look at only a few of those "pictures of God" in this discussion time.

1. Genesis 1:1. God was present when time began. He created all things. God made an orderly universe. Could creation have begun without God? Why or why not?

2. Exodus 34:1-7. What happened to the first list of command-ments? What did Moses do with them? Later, how is God described? Discuss the characteristics of God.

3. Deuteronomy 33:26-27. Who is like God? How powerful is He? How does God help us as our eternal refuge? What does Psalm 90:2 also say about God?

4. Psalm 139:1-24. How does God search us and "hem us in?" Can we get away from Him? Why not? Who has tried to do that? How and where can God lead us?

5. Isaiah 40:28-31. How is God described in these verses? Why doesn't the Creator become tired? What can God do for those who become exhausted? How?

6. John 4: 24. Who did Jesus talk to in this verse? What does it mean to worship God in spirit and in truth? How does true worship simplify what often seems to be complex?

7. Acts 17:22-31. Who is the Unknown God that Paul mentioned? Where does He live? What has He done? What command does God give to all people? Why?

8. Romans 11:33-36. Just when we think that some "theologians" know all about God, what does this verse tell them and us? Discuss every idea within this text.

9. 1 John 4:8-9. What one word is best used to describe or identify God? How did God demonstrate or prove His love to us? What does "atoning sacrifice" mean?

10. 1 Timothy 1:17; 6:13-16. What do the words mean about God being the King eternal, invisible and only God? What belongs to God forever? Are these words simple?

Gospel

—⟋⟍—

Second Kings chapter 7 tells the story of four lepers who sat at the entrance of the city of Samaria. Syrian soldiers had camped around the city and God's people, within the city, were dying from starvation. One of the lepers suggested that they go to the camp of the Syrians because it would not matter if the enemy killed them for they were dying of starvation as well as from leprosy.

When the four arrived near the camp of the Syrians, they discovered that their enemies had fled, leaving behind all their food stuff, and much more. The lepers devoured as much food as they wanted. Then one said that they had good news for their own Israelite people in Samaria, and they needed to go tell them. God's people had good news that day. They celebrated as they found food for and the Syrian enemies had gone.

We have the good news of the gospel to share with others. Many times we may be like the four lepers, not telling the story that is ours to share. Let's not keep it to ourselves, but tell everyone about the Savior who has come.

1. Isaiah 53:1-6. According to Isaiah, what is the message of the gospel? What did Christ do for those who believe, both Jews and Gentiles? Is there another gospel?

2. Luke 2:8-11. Why did shepherds near Bethlehem become filled with fear? What did an angel say to them? Who is the world's only Savior and what did He do?

3. Matthew 4:23-25. Where did Jesus begin His ministry? What is the gospel of the kingdom of heaven? What kind of work did Christ do? How did the people respond?

4. Romans 1:1. How did God call or set apart Paul for the gospel ministry? What did the prophets foretell about Jesus before He came? How can we share the gospel?

5. Romans 1:16. How did Paul show that he was not ashamed of the gospel? What is the gospel? Is there more than one gospel?

6. 1 Corinthians 15:1-5. What does the gospel do for the believer? What three basic elements compose the gospel? Name a few who first witnessed the gospel?

7. 1 Thessalonians 1:5. The gospel goes to people by preaching. What other ways does the gospel come to us? Explain.

8. Galatians 1:6-8. Name again the basic facts of the gospel. How is the gospel perverted? What does God say about those who declare "another gospel?"

9. Galatians 3:6-8. How did Abraham become righteous? How does God justify or make anyone righteous, Jew or Gentile? See Genesis 22:18.

10. 2 Thessalonians 1:8-9. When Christ returns, what will happen to those who have not accepted the gospel? What does it mean to be shut out from the Lord?

Grace

—⚡—

Early on the morning of December 8, 2005, this writer's son who lives in San Antonio, Texas, called his dad. The son knew something critical was wrong because he could only hear "mumbo jumbo." He told his wife, "Let's go. Something is wrong with dad." On the way to Laredo, he called the Sheriff's department and a hospital in that city. A deputy sheriff and an ambulance were dispatched to the small town east of the twin-cities on the Rio Grande. The ambulance driver and attendants found their man, and rushed him to a hospital in Laredo. A neurosurgeon "happened" to be in the emergency room, did a brain scan, drilled a hole to relieve the pressure on the brain, and then removed a blot clot. Two days later this writer said to the doctor in the I.C.U, "Doctor Estrada, you saved my life." He pointed his hand toward heaven indicating that life had come about by God's grace. Now this fellow has a new appreciation of grace. We don't know the depth of divine grace. The word means God's favor that no one deserves. The word expresses God's love and kindness for all people. Let's view the grace word.

1. Genesis 6:8. In the ancient world when man became evil, Noah found grace in God's eyes. Noah was blameless by God's grace. How does God's grace help us live?

2. Luke 2:40. At 12 years of age, Jesus was filled with wisdom and grace. What was the occasion of the text? What does it mean to say that Jesus grew in grace?

3. John 1:14, 17. Discuss the phrase, "The Word became flesh." Where was Jesus before He came to the earth? What does it mean that He was full of grace?

4. Acts 4:33. Much grace was upon the apostles. What if we would keep on giving witness to Christ's Resurrection, would God's grace be upon us too?

5. Romans 3:24. What does it mean to be justified? How much does justification cost the believer? Do we pay or work to be justified? What does redemption mean?

6. Romans 6:1. How bountiful is God's grace? Can we exhaust His grace? If we sin more, would that become a "bonus" for the Christian? What does Paul say?

7. 2 Corinthians 12:9. When tough times come, what's our hope? Why can we joyfully face tribulation that always encroaches upon us? What's the result of God's grace?

8. Ephesians 2:6-7. Why did God bring Jesus back to life again? What does it mean to speak of "future ages?" What incredible experience awaits us in the coming ages?

9. Hebrews 4:16. What does the throne of grace mean? How should we approach God's throne? What will be the result of going to God with confidence?

10. 2 Peter 3:18. Do most children grow physically? Is spiritual growth automatic? How can we grow in God's grace? Why should we want to grow in grace?

Health and healing

—ɱ—

Hospitals and health clinics are as numerous across America and the rest of the world as cactus and mesquite are in South Texas. People want to have good health, even though many never pay the price for this dream.

The Bible speaks in clear tones about the well-being of "saint and sinner." A study of a few Scriptures may hopefully help us see that God has interest in our total well-being.

1. Exodus 15:22-26. When the Israelites came out of Egypt, they found bitter water. How did it become sweet? Do you think that bitterness effects health? Why?

2. 2 Kings 2:21. What did Elisha do to change the bad water in Jericho? Can you name a few changes in life that would help people become healthy?

3. 2 Chronicles 7:14. What are important steps that must be taken for national healing? How would God help us if we were to follow His prescription?

4. Proverbs 3:7-8. What can bring health and nourishment to one's body? How? Do verses 5 and 6 hold a potential for better health? Why do you think so?

5. Isaiah 58:8. What are some elements in God's prescription for health? If you want to be healthy (although that's not always possible for some), what can you do?

6. Jeremiah 3:22. One spiritual illness is called backsliding. What does that mean? What is necessary for that kind of illness to be healed by the Lord?

7. Matthew 4:23. Why do you think Christ was able to heal? What illnesses are included in His healing power?

8. 1 Corinthians 12:9, 28, 30. What do you think of "diving healing?" Do some have the gift of healing? Why or why not? Who is the Healer? How does God heal?

9. James 5:16. Whose example in effective praying does James use? Do you think that praying for recovery can always be effective? Why or why not?

10. 3 John 1:2. Why do you think that John prayed that his friend would enjoy good health? Do you pray for the health of others? What is needed to be healthy?

Heaven

—∿—

A story or legend has circulated about a Christian who died. Upon arriving in heaven, an angel escorted him around the city. He felt tremendously impressed as he passed up and down the streets of gold. He gazed upon mansion after mansion, wondering when the angel would show him his palace. Finally they came to the outskirts of town and the angel stopped in front of a small cabin. As they started up the steps of the humble place, the Christian asked, "Why are we stopping here?" The angel said that this place was his. He wanted to know why he didn't have a palatial home, and not that place. The angel told him that the engineers had built his house out of the stuff that he had sent up before his arrival. What is heaven going to be like for each person? It might be that our eternal inheritance comes from what commitment and service to the Lord that we make while we travel the pilgrim's pathway.

1. 2 Kings 2:11. Elijah walked with Elisha and suddenly a fiery chariot and a wind swept that aged servant up to heaven. What reward do you think awaited him?

2. Matthew 6:19-21. We have certain needs where we live. What kinds of treasures can we "lay up" in heaven? Where is our heart when we send investments on ahead?

3. Luke 10:20. Christ's disciples had been on a mission. What exciting stories did they tell about when they returned? What other reason did they have for joy?

4. John 14:1-2. What did Jesus indicate that awaits His people beyond this life? Why has Jesus gone to heaven? What promise did the Savior give to His followers?

5. Acts 1:7-11. Do we know when Jesus will return? What mission is ours while we wait? How did Jesus go to heaven? What did two "visitors" tell the apostles?

6. Acts 7:51-56. Who was Stephen and why were religious leaders angry with him? What did he see? What did they do with Stephen? Who was one of his enemies?

7. 2 Corinthians 5:1. Why does God allow our earthly bodies to wear out? What does God have waiting for us in heaven? What kind of body will we have?

8. 2 Corinthians 12:1-4. Who did Paul write about in this text? What happened to him in the vision? Where is the "third heaven?" How did he describe heaven?

9. Hebrews 12:22-25. Describe some groups in heaven and what are they doing? What has Jesus done "once for all" for believers? What does verse 20 say?

10. Revelation 21:1-4; 22:1-5. Where does "the new heaven and new earth" come from? Who lives among His people? Why do you think heaven will be exciting?

Hell

—Ϻ—

Hell has always been a fearful, frightful word. What does it mean? Did Jesus teach about hell? What did He say about that topic?

A number of years ago, the late Dr. John Newport was teaching on the topic of "Last Things" in a large church in Houston, Texas. At the end of one of the sessions, some one said to him, "Dr. Newport, I didn't realize that people still believe in hell." The highly esteemed professor who had taught in several seminaries and universities, answered, "As far as I know, this doctrine is still in the Bible." Let's look at a few Scriptures that give some insight into the place where the unrighteous go at the end of this life or after judgment, if you prefer that phrase.

1. Isaiah 33:14. Why are sinners in Zion terrified? Why do the godless tremble? What does it mean to face "everlasting burnings?"

2. Matthew 5:21-22. What happens to those who commit murder, become angry with their brother, or says to another "you fool?" What do you think about hell?

3. Matthew 10:28. Why should we not be afraid of those who can kill us? Who should we fear? Why? What does "destroy" mean?

4. Matthew 18:7-9. What danger do people face who cause others to sin? What drastic action should any one do to avoid sin? What does it mean to pluck out the eye?

5. Matthew 25:41, 46. When Christ returns, what will He say to those on his left hand? What does that mean? What punishment will the unredeemed face?

6. Luke 16:19-31. Where was Lazarus placed each day? What happened to him and to the rich man? What requests did the rich man make? What answer did he hear?

7. 2 Thessalonians 1:9. When Jesus comes again, what will He say to those who have rejected Him? What does "everlasting destruction" mean?

8. James 3:6. What damage can the tongue cause? What is the source of the tongue's evil? What does it mean that the tongue is set on fire of hell?

9. 2 Peter 2:1-10. What do false religious teachers do? What happens to them? What did God do with sinning angels? What will God do with the unrighteous?

10. Revelation 20:12-15. Where do the lost appear when they are judged? What happens to those whose names are not in the book of life?

Help

—⚈—

Dr. Hoke Smith served as a missionary in Colombia and Argentina. One day his four-year old son came to him with a big apple, saying, "Daddy, help me get this apple started." We are like children who many times says, "Help me." The Bible speaks in clear language about the topic of helping. Look at some of these Scriptures.

1. Genesis 2:18. How may husbands and wives help each other? The wife helps her husband. They help one another. Why do we need helpers?

2. Deuteronomy 33:29. God's ancient people excelled all others. God became their helper. In what ways does this verse indicate that God helped them as well as us?

3. Job 6:13. We remember about Job when he faced trials. What were they? He didn't have strength to keep going. What happened to his resources? Who can help us?

4. Psalm 46:1. What does this Scripture tell us about God when troubles come? How is the Lord our "ever present help" in trying days of life? When do we need God?

5. Isaiah 41:10. Why do we not need to be fearful? Do you think God can help us with our problem-plagued lives? How is He able to help? In what areas do we need help?

6. Acts 16:9. Paul, Silas, Timothy, Luke, and others had engaged in mission activity. What did the people of Macedonia need from them? Do some call on you for help?

7. Romans 8:26. Sometimes we may be weak and can't pray. Why does the Holy Spirit want to help us? In what way does He help? When can we ask for the Spirit's help?

8. 1 Corinthians 12:28. What does the expression about "gift of helps" mean? How can we help others? Who are some people who need our help? Are we ready to help?

9. 2 Corinthians 1:11. Paul asked others to pray for him. In what ways did their praying help Paul? What was the response of some when Paul was helped?

10. Philippians 4:3. Among Paul's helpers, he named several ladies (Romans 16). How did they help Paul? How were they helped? Make a list of those you can help.

Holy Spirit

—∿—

The late Dr. A.J. Gordon, eminent Bible teacher, told of an Englishman visiting an American friend. The American said to him, "Come. Let me show you the greatest unused power in the world." When they looked at the Niagara Falls, the man from England said, "No, the greatest unused power in the world is the Holy Spirit."

In truth, The Holy Spirit is the spirit of power who wants to use believers for God's glory. We need to allow the Spirit of God to fill us and use us for His purposes. Let's review a few truths about the Holy Spirit that the Bible has for us.

1. Genesis 1: 2. The Holy Spirit "brooded over" a formless, void creation, described as like a hen setting over her eggs. The Spirit did a miraculous work, didn't He?

2. Genesis 6:1-6. How were people living in Noah's day? Why did God say that His Spirit would not always strive with man? Why is it dangerous to resist the Spirit?

3. Micah 3:8. Who was Micah? Why was he filled with power? How can we also be filled with the Holy Spirit? What difference will the fullness make within us?

4. Matthew 12:31-32. What is the sin against the Holy Spirit? Why can't that sin be forgiven? Do people commit that sin today? How?

5. Luke 4:16-19. Where was Christ when He "officially" began His ministry? What was the result of His being anointed by the Holy Spirit?

6. John 14:26. Who sent the Holy Spirit to live within the lives of God's people? When did that happen? What is one ministry of the Holy Spirit within us now?

7. John 16:8-11. What does this Scripture says the Holy Spirit is doing in the world today.? Why can't a person be converted without the Holy Spirit?

8. Acts 1:8. Why did Jesus tell the apostles to stay in Jerusalem? What happened to them when the Holy Spirit came? How does He equip us to be witnesses?

9. Acts 8:29. What was Philip doing when the Holy Spirit led him from Samaria? What did Philip then do? How does the Holy Spirit lead people to places of service today?

10. Romans 8:26. How does the Holy Spirit help us when we pray? Why do we need His help when praying? How do we discern and do God's will?

Humility

—〽—

John Newton, a converted slave trader in the 1700s, wrote the hymn, "Amazing Grace." When he was near death, a young pastor came to visit him, lamenting the fact that England was losing a great hymn writer and preacher. Newton told the visitor that he realized his life was coming to an end. Then he said to the young pastor, "If you look for me in heaven, you may find me at the feet of the thief on the cross who died believing in Jesus." The spirit of humility had engulfed the life of John Newton. Perhaps we need to place ourselves on that route, don't you think? About one person it has been said, "He can strut while sitting down." Let's see a few references about the theme of humility.

1. Deuteronomy 8:2-3. How did God humble the 12 tribes of Israel? During their years in the desert, what did they learn about bread? How do we learn that lesson?

2. Proverbs 16:18-19. What attitude does a person often have before he runs into a lot of trouble? What is better than sharing life with the proud?

3. Isaiah 57:15. What definition is given of God in this verse? Who can have fellowship with God? What benefits come to those who walk with God?

4. Micah 6:6-8. What does God require before a person presents sacrifices and offerings to Him? What does it mean to "walk humbly" with God?

5. Zechariah 9:9. How did Jesus demonstrate humility? How does that example apply today? What are some ways that we may identify a person who is humble?

6. Matthew 18:3. How did Jesus teach the meaning of humility? Why is one who humbles himself considered greatest in God's kingdom?

7. Luke 14:7-11. What choice of seats should one make on any special occasion? What could take place in the life of an humble person?

8. John 13:14-17. What did the disciples fail to do at the "Last Supper"? Why did they act as they did? What did Jesus do? How was that an act of humility?

9. Acts 20:19. How did Paul serve the Lord? What trials did he face? How do you think you would act under the circumstances which Paul constantly faced?

10. Philippians 2:5-8. How did Christ's birth show His humility? What relationship did He have with God? What was the crowning act of Christ's humility? Why?

Hunger or hungry

—⁓—

Often a young or older person may be seen on a busy thorough-
fare with a sign that reads, "Homeless and Hungry." What
may cause that person's unfortunate condition? Statistics indicate
that about two-thirds of the world's population go to bed hungry
every night. Some of those people sleep under bridges, in aban-
doned buildings, and in about any place that provides shelter from
heat or cold or other dangers. What should God's people do to help
the oppressed and suffering who may be near us?

1. Job 22:1-11. What false charges did Eliphaz bring against Job?
    How do some people help others without being noticed? How
    can we help the hungry today?

2. Psalm 146:5-9. Describe how God helps the hungry and
    oppressed. How do these words and actions apply to us? Do
    you think God wants us to follow His example?

3. Proverbs 19:15. Do problems come to certain elements of
    society because they refuse to work? What happens to a lazy
    and shiftless man? Should we help that person?

4. Isaiah 58:10-11. When does the Lord respond to His people?
    How can the hungry be helped? What benefits go to those who
    help the hurting?

5. Jeremiah 38:9-13. Who reported Jeremiah's condition to Judah's king? What kind of person do you think Ebed-Melech was? How can we reach out to the hungry?

6. Luke 4:1-2. How did Jesus suffer as He began His ministry? When He suffered from hunger, did Jesus complain? Are God's people exempt from hardships today?

7. Luke 6:25-26. What can take place in the lives of evil people who have an abundance? How do we learn to share with the unfortunate?

8. Luke 15:7. What did the prodigal son demand from his father? What did he do when he had spent or wasted all that he had? How can we help those who live foolishly?

9. 1 Corinthians 4:11. How can godly people suffer in their service to the Lord? How did Paul describe his difficulties as he served the Lord? How do some suffer today?

10. Revelation 7:16-17. In the future life, how will God alleviate hunger and other hardships from His people? Who will care for them then? How?

Husband

—ɯ—

One definition of a husband is that he is a man who plows. He takes care of his farm and crops. You know another definition of a husband. He is the man who "husbands" his wife and family. The Bible gives good instruction for husbands. Let's look at a few of the Bible references to find out if the husband is the kind of man he should be.

1. Genesis 2:18, 21-24. God said that it is not good for man to be alone. Why is this so? How did God solve the problem? Is marriage only between a man and woman?

2. 1 Samuel 1:8. Why was Elkanah disturbed? How did he try to comfort his wife? What did God do for their joy? How can husbands comfort their wives?

3. Proverbs 31:11, 23. Why should husbands have confidence in their wives? What blessing does the husband have when they get along well together?

4. Isaiah 54:5-7. Who wants to be the caretaker of the husband and wife? How does God show His concern for us? How does God's care of us give encouragement?

5. Jeremiah 3:20. Jeremiah refers to an unfaithful wife? Why is a wife unfaithful? How did Israel become unfaithful and what did God do as an example for us?

6.   Matthew 19:3-9. God's ideal for a husband and wife is that they never divorce. However, breakups happen. What answer do we have for marital problems?

7.   1 Corinthians 7:2-4. Why does God say that the husband and wife become one? Why should they love and be true to one another?

8.   Ephesians 5:22-25. How does Paul say that the husband is to love his wife? Is that a costly relationship? How would lasting love solve most marital problems?

9.   Colossians 3:19. Paul said the husband should not be harsh with the wife? How is harshness avoided? What takes place in the prayer life when either is harsh?

10.   1 Peter 3:7. Why should the husband be considerate of his wife? How is it shown? What gift do they share? What blessing flows from their healthy relationship?

Hypocrisy

—∿—

Hypocrites live all over planet earth, and suddenly we discover that in some ways, "They are us. Me!" A hypocrite is a person who says one thing and does something else. That one fails to keep his or her word. We don't practice what we preach. The original word meant "false face." The origin of the word had its roots in the Greek and Roman plays. The actors would wear masks. When the show or play ended, they would remove their masks, come down among the people, and live "normal lives."

Most ladies put on "make up" before going out in public. They want to look good. Men do similar things, too. Nothing is wrong with improving one's physical appearance. Women may say, "I need to have on more 'mascara'." In reality, that's a word relating to hypocrisy. In Spanish "mas" means more and "cara" means face. So they have more than their faces showing. Yes, we are all guilty of hypocrisy.

Jesus called many religious guys hypocrites. Let's view a few Scriptures that deal with this disturbing topic of hypocrisy.

1. Isaiah 29:13. Isaiah said people worshiped God with their lips and by rules, but not with their hearts. What about us? Jesus quoted Isaiah. (Matthew 15:7-9).

2. Ezekiel 33:30-32. God told Ezekiel that people in their houses said negative things about him. When they came to hear him, what did they do? What about today?

3. Matthew 6:2. Should we give to the needy? To Samaritan's Purse? What does this verse teach about helping others? What did the Pharisees do as they gave?

4. Matthew 6:4. Where is a good place to pray? Where are some places that we should not necessarily go when we pray? Why? How should we not pray?

5. Matthew 6:16-18. Does God approve of fasting? Why should people fast? If we go on a spiritual fast, how should we behave?

6. Matthew 6:13-15. Is evangelism one of the top priorities in God's business? When is so-called evangelism wrong? What did Jesus say about conversion practices?

7. Matthew 23:28-32. What did some teachers of the law do about the "outside of the cup?" What did they hide on the inside? Where was their "righteousness?"

8. Mark 12:15. What were some religious leaders trying to do with Jesus? How? What did they really want to do with Christ? What did Jesus call them?

9. 1 Timothy 4:1-5. What did Paul say many professing believers would do in the "last days" which began then? (Hebrews 1:2). How may such people be described?

10. 1 Peter 2:1. Why do garbage trucks pass by our houses or business places today? List some items in our lives that need to be thrown in the trash every day.

Inheritance

—⁓—

One of America's politicians married an heiress of a multi-billion dollar family business. He probably will never be standing on a street corner with a sign stating, "Homeless. Help me, please!" Many people have inherited fortunes across the centuries; many squander what they receive while others use their inheritance for the glory of God and the good of others. What about a spiritual inheritance that lasts forever? Do we have an electrifying interest in what God can give us that has everlasting value? Let's take a look at some Scriptures which give insight into God's promises that never come to an end.

1. Exodus 34:9-14. Moses prayed that God would forgive the wickedness of the Israelites and take them as His heritage. God's response amazes us, doesn't it?

2. Job 27:13. Job sometimes felt overwhelmed at the prosperity of evil people. Then he declared that they inherit the wind. What does that mean? Can you hold the wind?

3. Psalm 119:111. David wrote that God's Scriptures became his inheritance forever. The Word of God gave him joy. How? Why should the Bible be our heritage?

4. Psalm 127:3. Do you think that children are an inheritance from God? Why are parents blessed who have children? How can children be blessed by parents?

5. Proverbs 20:21. Solomon says we should not be lazy. (Hush, man!). He says imitate those who through patience and faith inherit God's promises. How can we?

6. Matthew 25:34. If we do a full-fledged ministry as this text indicates, what blessings will come to us? Who is preparing an inheritance for those who help others?

7. Luke 15:12. The prodigal son demanded of his father his inheritance. How can parents teach children to be careful with their heritage, though small or great?

8. Romans 14:13-14; (Hebrews 11:8ff). How did Abraham receive his inheritance? How is he the father of all who believe? What inheritance awaits us?

9. Ephesians 5:1-7. Who are some on the immoral list? Why can't they receive an inheritance from God? (Revelation 22:14). How can anyone receive an inheritance?

10. 1 Peter 3:9. In what ways does Peter challenge believers to live with each other? What kind of "grades" do you think we are getting today? What blessing awaits us?

Jesus Christ — His humanity

—ɯɯ—

Today more than six billion people live on the face of the earth. We call those who live on this planet human beings. That is, each one is a part of the big "human family."

For centuries questions have been debated about the humanity as well as the deity of Jesus. Is Christ both human and divine? The Bible calls Jesus "Son of man" as well as "Son of God." Which is He, divine or human? The biblical answer is that Jesus is both: He is God as well as man, now glorified. Eternally, He is God. For two thousand years, Jesus has also been a human being. At this time of discussion, let's think about a few references which tell about the humanity of Jesus.

1. Isaiah 7:14. One of the earlier prophecies about Jesus relates to His physical birth. About 700 years before Christ was born, what did Isaiah write about that birth?

2. Matthew 1:1. What does the word genealogy mean? Who were two prominent "forebears" of Jesus? What does this ancestral line tell about Jesus?

3. Matthew 1:18-25. Who was the mother of Jesus? Did He have a human father? What is another name of Jesus? Who became the husband of Mary?

4. Matthew 4:1-11. What is another proof of the humanity of Jesus? Who tempted Jesus and in what ways did temptations come to Him? Are we tempted?

5. Matthew 8:20. What do foxes and birds have that Jesus did not have when He lived on this earth? How was Christ qualified to identify with the poor and outcast?

6. Matthew 9:6-13. Do human beings eat? Where was Jesus when He ate with "publicans and sinners?" How did that "dinner date" show Christ's humanity?

7. Matthew 26:26-45. What did the disciples do when Christ was praying in Gethsemane? How did that experience prove the humanity of Jesus?

8. Luke 2:40. What happened to Jesus between the age of 12 and 30? How does that indicate His humanity? How did Jesus grow during that time in His life?

9. Mark 15:34-37. What happened to Jesus while He was on the cross? Why do you think God left Christ alone or forsook Him? Did His death show His humanity?

10. 1 John 1:1-4; 4:2-3. What are some ways that Jesus related to His followers that prove His humanity? What about those who deny that Jesus has come in the flesh?

Jesus Christ — His deity

—〰—

S omeone asked the writer Schalom Asch who came to the USA
from Poland in 1905 how he could write a book on Jesus entitled *The Nazarene*, since he himself was a Jew. Mr. Asch responded
by saying that he had read books from notable authors from earliest
times and had known many great writers of his generation, but he
said that he had never met or known about anyone as great as Jesus
who many called the Christ.

Most of the world faces a critical problem. The crisis revolves
around Jesus. Who is He? The Evangelical world believes that Jesus
is God who has come in the flesh. That is, Jesus is human as well
as fully divine. Why do we declare that Christ is the divine Son of
God? The entire Bible supports this truth. Let's look at a few of the
dozens of Scriptures declaring that Christ is God as well as man..

1. Micah 5:2. The Hebrew text should be followed. That prophet
    said that Christ would be born in Bethlehem. His movements
    are from everlasting. What does this teach?

2. Luke 22:66-71. What did the religious leaders ask Jesus? Who
    did He confess that He was? How did they feel about Jesus?
    What immediately followed?

3. John 1:1-2. What does "the beginning" mean? How theologi-
    cally can the "Word" be defined? What partnership did Jesus
    have at that time with God?

4. John 1:29-34. What testimony did John the Baptist give of Jesus? What did He say about "the Lamb of God?" Is man able to cleanse himself of His sin? Who can?

5. John 10:30; 34-39. How did Jesus identify Himself with God? What do those words mean? What kind of a conflict erupted between Jesus and religious leaders?

6. Romans 1:4. This verse links Jesus to David, showing Christ's humanity. What did God do with His Son who was crucified? What does Christ provide for His people?

7. Colossians 2:9. What does this verse say about the fullness of God in Christ? What does this statement show about Jesus? What position does Jesus now have?

8. Hebrews 1:1-4. How did God first speak to His people. In these "last days," how has God spoken to the world? How does this Scripture describe Christ? Is He an angel?

9. 1 Peter 2:21-23. How long did Simon Peter and the other apostles live with Jesus? Did any of them ever point out any wrong in his life? What did Peter say of Him?

10. Revelation 1:8; 17:14; 19:16 (Isaiah 44:6; 45:18). The Bible states that God is the Alpha and Omega and the Lord of lords. Why does Jesus have those titles?

Jesus Christ — His death

—ɯ—

History has recorded the deaths of many of the world's greatest philosophers, scientists, inventors, teachers, and religious leaders. The death of Jesus forever holds first place among those who have died across the centuries. Any one who tries to deny the birth and death of Jesus overlook the plain facts of the Bible and human history. The Bible presents the case of the death of Jesus over and over again. The Old Testament prophesized Christ's death. He Himself told of His death. The New Testament has evidence indisputable about the pre-existence, birth, life, death, and ascension of Christ. Let's see briefly some of the evidence that indicates that Christ died so that His followers might have life everlasting.

1. Isaiah 53:5-8. Isaiah states that Jesus was pierced and crushed for our iniquities. He was led as a sheep to the slaughter. What do these expressions mean?

2. Matthew 20:17-19. What did Jesus tell His disciples on the way to Jerusalem? What were the Gentiles going to do with Him? How do you think the apostles felt?

3. Matthew 27:35-50. While Christ was being crucified, what did some say or shout to Him? What were Christ's words in a loud voice? What does verse 50 state?

4. Luke 22:19-20. What did Jesus teach His apostles about His death at the Last Supper? What did the bread represent? What did the wine indicate?

5. Luke 24:45-47. What did Christ say about His sufferings? What did that suffering mean? After His resurrection, what were the apostles commissioned to do?

6. John 3:14. What did Moses do for the people who had been bitten by snakes? What did his lifting up the serpent on a pole signify?

7. John 10:17-20. Was Christ forced to die? Did He have to die? How did He die? What reaction did the Jews have when Jesus spoke to them?

8. Acts 2:22-24. How did Jesus accredit Himself among His own people and nation, as well as among the Gentile world? Who crucified Him? Then what happened?

9. Acts 17:1-4. When Paul entered Thessalonica, what did he do for three sabbaths? What response did the Jews make to Paul's preaching about Jesus?

10. 1 Thessalonians 5:9-10. Why did Jesus die for us? What gift did God appoint for us to receive? What does salvation mean to you?

Jesus Christ — His resurrection

—∽—

An ancient legend tells of a bird called the Phoenix. According to the legend, the bird lived to be 500 years of age. When he died, flames devoured his body, and from the ashes another Phoenix came forth and repeated the process. What is true and not legend is the resurrection of Jesus. The stories of Jesus are fact, not fiction. Let's look at what the Bible states are infallible proofs of Christ's resurrection. Acts 1:3 tells of Christ's resurrection and is the only verse in the Bible that uses the word "infallible."

1. Psalms 16:9-10. (Acts 13:34-35). God promised not to leave Christ's body in what place? What would not happen to His body and where would Christ be?

2. Matthew 20:17-19. What did Jesus say would happen to Him when He arrived in Jerusalem? After being mocked, flogged, and crucified what would happen to Him?

3. Matthew 28:1-15. What women arrived at the place of Christ's burial? What did an angel show them? Who soon greeted them? Why were Roman soldiers bribed?

4. Luke 24:13-46. Who walked sadly along the road to Emmaus on the day of Christ's resurrection? How did Christ show them that He was alive?

5. John 2:18-22. What did the Jews want Jesus to do to prove His authority? How did they misunderstand His words? When did the disciples remember those words?

6. John 20:19-28. Where did 10 of the disciples meet on the Sunday evening after Christ's resurrection? How did Jesus appear to them and what did He do?

7. Acts 1:3. How many "infallible proofs" of Christ's resurrection can you name? New Testament believers had full evidence of Christ's victory over death. Do we doubt it?

8. Romans 8:31-34. What does it mean that God did not spare His own Son? After His death, what did Paul say happened to Jesus? What is He doing for us now?

9. 1 Corinthians 15:1-8. Paul said that Christ died, was buried, and rose from the grave. Who were some who saw the resurrected Christ? How many saw Christ at one time?

10. Revelation 1:17-18. John saw Jesus several years after His ascension. Why did Jesus tell John not to be afraid? Should we be fearful of death? Why or why not?

Jesus Christ — His return

—⟋𝔪⟍—

About two thousand years ago, Jesus came to this earth as the son of God and the son of the Virgin Mary. He came in fulfillment of Old Testament prophecies.

The Bible states that Jesus is going to come again or return. Dozens of references in both the Old Testament and the New Testament state clearly that Jesus is going to return. Just as people in the first century did not understand everything about His first coming, in similar fashion we do not know everything about Christ's return. Jesus stated that He as well as the angels in heaven didn't know everything about His coming again. Therefore we should not claim to know all about that glorious return of Christ. One fact is clear: Jesus is going to return. Let's look at a few specific facts about His coming again.

1. Daniel 7:13. When Daniel had visions at night of the return of Jesus, what will be given to Jesus? How is He coming? What about the kingdom of God?

2. Matthew 24:29-31. When did Jesus say that He would return? Did He say that He would go to heaven and return after seven years? What happens to the elect or saved?

3. John 14:1-3. What did Jesus say He would do for His people when He returned to heaven following His death and resurrection? Then what promise did He make?

4. Acts 1:7-11. What did the apostles do as Christ ascended to heaven? What did Moses and Elijah tell the apostles? (possibly them: Matthew 17:3) See v. 7.

5. Acts 3:19, 21. What is one way unbelievers as well as believers can prepare for Christ's return? Do we understand what Christ will do when He comes again?

6. 1 Corinthians 4:5. Why should we be careful about judging others before Christ returns? What will be another mission of Jesus when He comes again?

7. 1 Corinthians 15:24-26. Who gets final control over the kingdom of God? What will be the final enemy that Jesus will destroy?

8. 1 Thessalonians 3:13; Jude 1:14. What was Paul's prayer? Is it being fulfilled? Who was Enoch (Genesis 5:24)? What did he prophecy?

9. 1 Thessalonians 4:16-17. What happens to the bodies of believers who have died when Christ returns? What happens to the living saints?

10. 1 John 3:2. What is the meaning of the statement that we will be like Jesus when He returns? What will we be doing if we have the hope of seeing and being like Jesus?

Joy

—⁓—

Everyone wants to be happy and joyful. We spend money on houses, cars, vacations, etc. because we think that things give us joy. God wants us to have His joy. Heaven will be a place of joy. As Christians, we should let the joy of the Lord fill us. Hundreds of verses of Scripture tell of joy. Let's consider ten of those references.

1. Nehemiah 8:10. After rebuilding the walls of Jerusalem, Nehemiah told the Hebrews to celebrate with food and drink. What gave them strength? How does joy help us?

2. Psalm 51:12. Why did David ask God to restore the joy of his salvation? How does a person lose joy? What's the route to restore joy? How does salvation give joy?

3. Proverbs 23:24-25. What happens in the life of a man who has a righteous son? How does a father feel about a wise son? How do parents of a godly person feel?

4. Isaiah 61:10. What kind of joy does a believer have in God? What are some benefits that a person has who trusts in the Lord? Why should we always rejoice in the Lord?

5. Jeremiah 15:16. What did the prophet do with God's Word? What does eating God's Word mean? What blessing does a person have who fills life with the Bible?

6. Habakkuk 3:18. What kind of tough times did Habakkuk and others face in their day? What reaction did he have? What's our response to difficulties?

7. Zephaniah 3:17. According to Zephaniah, what is God able to do for His people? What action does God take over His people? Why does God rejoice over us?

8. Luke 24:50-53. What did Jesus do about 40 days after His resurrection? Who was with Him? How did the disciples feel and what did they do?

9. 1 Peter 1:8. What specific action do believers take in relation to Jesus, even though we have not seen Him? How is a Christian's joy described? Do you have this joy?

10. Jude 1:24. What did Jude say that Jesus would do for believers when He returns? What will be Christ's attitude toward His people when He comes again?

Justify or justification

—〰—

One of the words in the New Testament that is hard to understand or define is justification. Some have tried to simplify the word by stating that justification means "just as if I had never sinned." This definition puts the word closer to our understanding. However, justification actually means to make or declare righteous. The struggle goes on with the understanding of the word. Can man by his works make himself right with God? Does justification come by faith and works? How is one justified? Let's see what the Bible says about justification.

1. Genesis 15:6. Moses wrote that Abraham believed God and that belief was counted unto him for righteousness? If belief leads to obedience, how is one justified?

2. Job 25:4-6. Job asked a great question: How can a man be righteous before God? If the stars are not pure in God's sight, what about man? Let's look at more Scripture.

3. Luke 16:15. The Pharisees looked with contempt upon Jesus. He said they endeavored to justify themselves before one another. Who really knows us?

4. Acts 13:39. Paul knew the meaning of justification. He wrote that those who believe are justified by faith, not by the Law. What's your reaction to his declaration?

5.   Romans 3:19-26. Does God declare a person righteous who tries to keep the law? Why not? How does this text state that a person becomes righteous or justified?

6.   Romans 5:1. What is the deeper meaning of being justified by faith? Faith in what or whom? What is the result of justification? Why does everyone need God's peace?

7.   1 Corinthians 6:9-11. What kinds of people in the Corinthians church had been saved or redeemed by Christ? How are the lost washed, sanctified, and justified?

8.   Galatians 3:1-14; 23-29. One of the great passages of Scripture that deserve much study is this one. What is the benefit from the law? How is one justified?

9.   Titus 3:4-7. Why are we not redeemed by our own works or deeds? How does God save us? What happens to the one who is justifed by grace? Elaborate.

10.   James 2:24-25. Does this Scripture contradict other verses that tell of Abraham's justification? Do these words mean that Abraham proved his faith by his works?

Kingdom of God

—∿—

The basic meaning of "kingdom" is the territory over which a king rules. A broader definition of that word is often understood as a nation or country. Statistics indicate that more than 150 nations are in the world. This number varies as revolutions occur and nations break apart.

God's kingdom is one, even though struggles continue among a few groups within the Lord's everlasting kingdom. When Jesus comes again, man's "worldly kingdom" will come to a close, the devil's doings will soon thereafter be shut down, and everything according to God's plan will come beneath His umbrella. We should not be overly concerned about the details of when and how God will take final control of the world's empires. God's people should be satisfied to say, "Lord, your will be done." Meanwhile, let's take a look at some Scriptures that deal with God's kingdom or His rule.

1. Exodus 19:6. What plan did God have for the ancient Israelites when He called them? Do Christians inherit that responsibility? See 1 Peter 2:5 and Revelation 1:6.

2. 1 Chronicles 29:10-14. Discuss David's prayer. What did he say about God? Who is the head of God's kingdom? How does David say we can share in the kingdom?

3. Daniel 4:3; 7:27. What kind of kingdom does God have? What will God eventually do with worldly kingdoms? What will rulers do when Christ returns?

4. Luke 9:57-62. What did some would-be followers of Jesus hear Him say? Then what did some say about following Jesus? What did Jesus say to those who look back?

5. Luke 17:21. Where is the kingdom of God today in relation to God's people? What does that mean? Does God rule over our lives as King today? How?

6. John 3:3, 7. If one wants to see the kingdom of God now, what must first take place in that one's life? What is necessary for one to enter the kingdom of God?

7. John 18:36-37. What do you think it means that Christ's kingdom is not of this world? How did Jesus answer Pilate's question about His being a King?

8. Romans 14:17. What kind of kingdom is God's kingdom if it is not "meat and drink?" Name and discuss three characteristics of those in God's kingdom?

9. Hebrews 12:28. What kind of kingdom do the people of God inherit? What should be our attitude since we are in His kingdom? How are we to worship the Lord?

10. Revelation 11:12. Loud voices will be heard as Christ returns. What will then happen to worldly kingdoms? What will Christ then do? (1 Corinthians 15:24).

Lies and lying

—m—

Charles Colson served as presidential aide to former President Richard Nixon. Several years later because of his prison experience, Colson founded the international ministry Prison Fellowship. Among the many books he wrote is one entitled *Lies That Go Unchallenged*. The problem of lying respects no person. However, the Bible speaks clearly about speaking falsehood. Look at a few of the many references to lying that may be studied.

1. Judges 16:10, 13. Who was Samson and who was Delilah? Was it wrong for Samson to deceive her about the secret of his strength? Is it always wrong to lie? Why?

2. Psalm 58:3. What does this verse teach us about sin? How does a person learn to tell lies? Is there a way to win victory over falsehood?

3. Psalm 101:7. This verse has a reference to God's attitude toward those who don't tell the truth. Does God welcome falsifiers into His presence? Why or why not?

4. Proverbs 25:18. Can we harm a person by telling falsehoods about that one? If we lie about a person, the damage is compared to hurting him or her in what ways?

5. Jeremiah 14:14-15. Who were the false prophets? What did the false prophets tell the people? What punishment would they receive? Do such prophets live today?

6. John 8:44. Who did Jesus say is "the father of lies? Can you think of one lie that the devil has told? (See Genesis 3). How long has the devil been twisting the truth?

7. Acts 5:3-4. What did Ananias and Sapphira tell Simon Peter? Did they have to give all their possessions to the early Church? Why did they lie? What happened to them?

8. Romans 9:1-3. What did Paul seek continually to do? What did he say about his passion to win the unbelieving Jews? What can we honestly say is our passion?

9. 1 John 1:6. Do we like to have fellowship with Jesus? What does fellowship with Jesus mean? If we walk in spiritual darkness, what are we doing?

10. Revelation 21:27. Can those who practice telling lies enter into heaven? What is the hope for those who do not speak and live the truth?

Life

A humorous story tells of three men who mentioned how they would like to be remembered when they died. The first said he would like for people to say about him that he had been a hard-working man, that he had been a good husband and father, and that everyone hated to lose him as their friend. The second one had a similar story. He wanted people to say about him that he was honest, had been going to church all his life, and he had been a role-model family man. The third one said that when people came by to view his body, one person would suddenly exclaim, "Look! He's breathing!"

This thought-provoking study relates to spiritual life that "keeps breathing." We can learn from the Scriptures that we don't have to die, but with Christ in the heart we will live forever. Hopefully from what the Bible teaches we can have a greater appreciation for the spiritual life that each person receives through faith in Jesus.

1. Genesis 2:7, 9. When God created man, he didn't leave him as a clod of dirt. He became a living soul. God also provided the "tree of life." Comments?

2. Matthew 7:13-14. What kind of road leads to eternal life? What road leads to death? What road do most people travel? Why? Which way is open to everyone?

3. Luke 18:29-30. This verse does not refer to salvation by works. The disciples believed in Jesus. What will people receive because of total commitment?

4. John 3:14-16. What does verse 14 refer to? See Numbers 21:8-9. Why was Jesus "lifted up?" What does this mean? What must a person do to have eternal life?

5. John 5:24. What does it mean to hear Christ's words? What does it mean to believe in God? What did God do? What takes place in the life of one who believes?

6. John 10:10-11. What does a thief do? What is the contrast between Jesus and a thief? What is the more abundant life? What price did Christ pay for our lives?

7. John 11:21-44. How long had Lazarus been dead when Jesus arrived? What did Jesus say in verse 25? What did Jesus say to Lazarus? What does He say to us?

8. Colossians 3:1-3. If we have life in Christ, where should our interests be found? Where is our life hidden? What will take place with us when Jesus comes again?

9. 2 Timothy 1:10. Who is our Savior? Why has Jesus appeared? Has Christ won the victory over physical and spiritual death? How has immortal life come to us?

10. 1 John 3:14. What does it mean to pass from death to life? What about those who do not believe in Jesus? How do we know that we are alive spiritually?

Light

—ɯ—

Scientists say that light travels at about 185,000 miles per second. Light from the sun reaches the earth in about seven minutes. One way to explain light is to say that it is the absence of darkness. Since spiritual light is the absence of evil it is evident that we live in a dark world morally and spiritually except for the pockets of light that shine where God's people may be. Let's let the Bible give some insights into the subject of light.

1. Genesis 1:3-5. God created light. He gave us the day for light and the night for darkness. God saw the light that it was good? What do you think of darkness?

2. Isaiah 9:2. Who were the people walking in darkness? What shone upon those who lived in the shadow of death? What was the light that came to those in darkness?

3. Isaiah 42:6. Why did God call the Israelite nation into His light? What does it mean that God's people became a light to the Gentiles? Who can share God's light now?

4. Matthew 5:14-16. What role do God's people play in the world? What are we like? What two reasons are stated for our spiritual lights to shine?

5. John 5:35. What do you know of John the Baptist? With what did Jesus compare John? What is necessary for a lamp to give light? How can we burn for Jesus?

6. John 8:12. What unique claim did Jesus make about Himself? What happens to His followers? Do all believers walk in light? If so, what do they have?

7. 2 Corinthians 4:6. Where did light come from? Why does God let His light shine in our hearts? Why or how do we learn more of God's light and glory through Jesus?

8. Philippians 2:14-15. How should Christians behave if they are to give spiritual light in the world? What kind of world are we living in? How can we shine like stars?

9. 1 John 1:5-6. What is one definition of God? How is God giving light to each of us? Can a person have fellowship with God and live in darkness? Why or why not?

10. Revelation 22:5. What splendor will fill heaven for eternity? Why won't we need the light of the sun, moon, stars, or some electrical company in "the sweet by and by?"

Love — 1 Corinthians 13

—⟋⟍—

Several years ago, Professor Henry Drummond of Oxford University became a believer after hearing Evangelist Dwight L. Moody preach in a crusade in London. Dr. Drummond left his teaching post in the university, and began to tell everyone about what Christ had done for him. Later he wrote a book on 1 Corinthians chapter 13 entitled "The Greatest Thing In the World." Let's look at the verses in this love chapter.

1. 1 Corinthians 13:1. Some who speak eloquently may be compared to what instruments if they don't love? What do you think of unrefined noise?

2. 1 Corinthians 13:2. If a person has the gift of prophecy and has a full quota of wisdom, but lacks love, how may that one be defined?

3. 1 Corinthians 13:3. If anyone gives generously to the poor and is willing to sacrifice his or her body for a cause and does not have love, what does that one gain?

4. 1 Corinthians 13:4. What six words in verse 4 describe love? Talk about these qualities of love.

5. 1 Corinthians 13:5-7. Love expresses itself in what kind of actions? Which is the more important expression in this list?

6.   1 Corinthians 13:8. How long does love last? Who came as the full embodiment or expression of love?. How did Jesus show that love?

7.   1 Corinthians 13:8-12. What are some noble qualities in the present life that are "fluff" in comparison to love that is eternal?

8.   1 Corinthians 13:13. Name three qualities of the Christian life that have significance. Why do you think these virtues or aspects of life are important?

9.   1 Corinthians 13:13. Why do you think that love is greater than faith and hope? Does the fact that love is supreme reduce the value of faith and hope? Why?

10.   1 Corinthians 13:1-13. Do you think your life would change by reviewing this chapter each day for a week or month? Will you make this experiment?

Love — number two

—ɯ—

During the early ministry of D.L. Moody, a young boy rode a trolley across town to attend the evangelist's Sunday School class. When asked why he made a long trip to be with that particular group, he answered, "Because they love little boys like me over there."

The Bible mentions love hundreds of times. Paul says that love is the greatest mark of a Christian. Look at a few references to love in this time that this topic is studied.

1. Deuteronomy 6:5-6. What are the first attention-getting words in this Scripture? What is the three-dimensional love we should have for God? How do we prove it?

2. 1 Samuel 18:1-4. Jonathan was the son of King Saul who hated David. How did Jonathan show his love for David? How do we show love to others?

3.   Proverbs 10:12. What does hatred cause? What action does love take? How does it cover sin? How many sins? What sins? What reaction is yours to this verse?

4. Song of Solomon 8:6-7. What does it mean that love is like a seal over the heart? How does love act? What is unable to quench love? Is love greater than wealth?

5. Matthew 5:44. Who does Jesus say we are to love? Do families and nations have enemies? How can we show them our love? Are we carrying out this command?

6. Luke 10:25-37. What did a teacher of the law ask Jesus? What answer did he hear? How are we to love God? What did Jesus say about one's neighbor?

7. John 17:34-35. What did Jesus give His followers? How are we to love? What is the result when we love one another? Do we practice these words? Why or why not?

8. Ephesians 3:17-19. Do you feel that you are "rooted and established in love?" What does this mean? How is Christ's love described? How does love surpass knowledge?

9. 1 Thessalonians 3:12. What is your idea of making love increase? If love overflows for each other, what will be the result in family life, community life, etc?

10. 1 John 4:16-18. How can we describe God? If we love, where does God live and what is our address? What is the result of perfect love?

Love — number three

—⚏—

Although most of us do not know anything about the Greek language, we may find three words in that language which express love. Eros is a sensual love, quite often meaning that which is devoid of real love. The second word is fileo which generally means a friendly love. The highest kind of love is agape or divine love, although fileo or friendship love and divine love sometimes are interchangeable.

In John 21:15 and following, Jesus asked Peter if he loved Him with agape love. Simon Peter answered Jesus two times that he loved Him with fileo or friendship love. The third time Jesus asked Peter that question saying, "Peter do you even love me with a friendship love?" That's why Peter felt sad. We should search our hearts and ask ourselves if we love one another and especially Christ with the highest love.

1. Genesis 22:2. What did an angel say to Abraham? How did Abraham prove his love to God? (Hebrews 11:19). How do we prove our love for our children?

2. Genesis 29:18. How did Jacob show his love for Rachel? Then what happened? How do you show your love for your wife or husband? Be honest!

3. Isaiah 38:17. How did God show His love for Isaiah as well as for Israel? What did God do for the sins of His people? How did He do that? How grateful are you?

4.   Matthew 22:35-40. Why did a religious leader ask Jesus which was the greatest commandment? What answer did Jesus give? What do you think of Jesus' answer?

5.   Matthew 24:12. What causes people's love to grow cold? How can dying love be revived? If our love is real, how does it express itself to God and to others?

6.   John 13:34-35. Why did Jesus say He was giving a new commandment? What does it mean to love as Jesus does? How do unbelievers know we are Christians?

7.   Romans 5:5. What does it mean that God has poured his love into our hearts? How does God do this? Can we experience God's love every day? Do we?

8.   Romans 13:10. How does love express itself to one's neighbor? Are there exceptions? Why or why not? How do we fulfill the law?

9.   1 Thessalonians 5:12-13. What does it mean to have someone in charge or over us in the Lord? Why should we hold in high esteem those who work among us?

10. 1 John 4:16-18. What is one way to describe God? What does it mean that love is made complete in us? What does perfect love do?

Memory

—⟪⟫—

Some scientific investigations state that goldfish have a memory of three seconds. Praise the Lord that He made us with a memory that outdistances that beautiful fish. You and I remember many experiences from childhood to the present — our parents, work, schooling, friends, and much more. Some memories are wonderful, and some may be a *nightmare*. The Bible speaks quite frequently to us, saying, *Remember*!

1. Numbers 15:38. God gave clothing assignments to Israel's priests. They were to dress appropriately. Why did they have *tassels* on their clothes?

2. Nehemiah 4:14. What message did God give to Israel through Nehemiah? Who would do their battles? Did God use His people? Who were they to remember?

3. Psalm 63:6. Where and when does a person need to remember God? Why should we remember God as our Shepherd? If this is so, what takes place in life?

4. Ecclesiastes 12:1. When should a person remember his or her Creator? Do you think young people keep God in the center of their thoughts? Why should we?

5. Jonah 2:7. Where was Jonah when he prayed? What could have happened to him? Do you ever feel as Jonah did with a *fainting spell*? Why? What's the answer?

6. Zechariah 10:9. God said that He would chasten His people by sending them into far-away countries because of their sin. What would they do then? What about us?

7. Matthew 26:6-13. Let someone tell the story of the sinful woman mentioned in this text. Why was she criticized? What did Jesus say about that event?

8. Luke 16:19-31 Discuss the two men in this story. What happened to the beggar? What about the other man? What two words did he hear? What does this mean?

9. Luke 22:14-20. When and where did the "Last Supper" take place? What did the bread and wine represent? Do we remember Jesus as we celebrate His supper?

10. John 2:22. Why did Jesus expel money changers? What did He say about His authority for that action? When did the disciples remember that event?

Mercy

—⚒—

To understand mercy, we need to study Exodus 25:10-22. When Israel came out of Egypt, God asked them to build a tabernacle where His people could worship. The Ark of the Covenant was placed inside the Holy of Holies. The ark was like a cedar chest, about the size of a communion table. The 10 commandments were kept inside the ark, thus it was called "The Ark of the Covenant." The top of the ark was called the "mercy seat" because God's presence especially dwelled there. Once a year the Great High Priest sprinkled blood on the covering of the ark, indicating that the sins of the people had been covered. The ark's top or lid was called God's "mercy seat" because He showed mercy to His people when He saw the blood sprinkled on it. God's mercy is mentioned 148 times in the Old Testament and various times in the New Testament.

1. Nehemiah 9:19-21. God blessed Israel for 40 years in the desert. What did God do about their food, water, clothes, shoes, heat and cold? How is mercy shown now?

2. Proverbs 28:13. What happens to one who refuses to confess sin? How does God show mercy to those who admit their wrong? Is confession to be offensive?

3. Lamentations 3:21-23, 22. What does the text mean that says God's mercies are new every morning? How are God's mercies life-sustaining?

4. Micah 7:18. How does this verse surprise you? Who may receive God's mercies? How does God feel about showing mercy to us? Memorize these four words.

5. Luke 10:37-38. Is mercy mostly a doctrine and creed or is it a practice? How does this Scripture illustrate true mercy? Where can we discover places to show mercy?

6. Romans 12:1. God calls upon His people to live consecrated lives. What is the basis for our commitment to God? Without God's mercies, could we live for His glory?

7. Romans 12:8. Mercy is a gift from God. How can we cultivate this gift? How do we demonstrate mercy? Do we show mercy with cheerfulness or by grumbling?

8. Ephesians 2:4. Grace means the undeserved kindness and favor of God. How does God show the riches of His grace? See the book of Jonah. How rich is His grace?

9. Titus 3:5-7. Does this verse teach salvation by rituals or good deeds that a person may do? How is God's mercy shown in this text? How does Jesus save us?

10. Hebrews 2:17; 4:16. What kind of a high priest is Jesus? How did Jesus become our high priest? How do we receive God's mercy? What does this mean for us?

Now

—◁◁▷◁▷—

Quite often we use the word "now." The dictionary defines now as an adverb of time. We like to eat now. We want to have a new house, car, or bigger salary now. We don't like to wait to checkout in grocery lines — we want out now. However, we may be something like the person who wrote the following lines: "Procrastination is my sin; It brings me nothing but sorrow. I think to rid myself of it; I think I will — tomorrow!" Let's think of having good experiences *now* as followers of Jesus.

1. John 9:25. What did Jesus do for a blind man, and what did he then start doing? (9:1-25). What did he say to his critics? Do you have that blind man's assurance?

2. John 15:3. Who heard the words of Jesus about cleansing? In what way does God's Word make us clean? Does this verse apply to us now? How?

3. John 15:22. What did the message of Christ do for unbelievers? Do you think anyone now has an excuse for his or her sin? How can we handle the sin problem?

4. 2 Corinthians 5:20. According to the text, what "office" do God's people have? When do we tell others of reconciliation? Are you one of Christ's ambassadors?

5. 2 Corinthians 6:2. When is the time of God's favor? When is the day of salvation? Is it wise to wait in receiving Jesus as Savior? Why or why not?

6. Galatians 2:20. What did the apostle Paul say happened to him? What does "being crucified" mean? How does a Christian live now or today after being crucified?

7. Colossians 3:8. What kind of ugly attitudes and actions should Christians put aside? When? Are we daily ridding ourselves of that which the Bible says "throw out?"

8. Hebrews 9:24-26. What did Christ do after His death and resurrection? What is He doing for believers in heaven now? What is He *not* doing there for us now?

9. 1 John 2:18. When did the "last hour" (days) begin (Hebrews 1:2). Who is active in the world according to this text? Who is an antichrist and what does he do?

10. 1 John 3:2. What happens to a person who receives Christ as Savior? When does a believer become God's child? What will Christ do for believers when He returns?

Patience

—◊—

We have heard the expression, "That person has 'the patience of Job'." The basic definition of patience is to stay beneath the load without letting the knees buckle. The Greek word is upomeno. Upo is a prefix meaning under. Meno means "I abide or remain." What is your experience with patience? Look at some Scripture passages that deal with the virtue of patience.

1. Psalm 40:1-3. This verse reminds us that sometimes we need to wait on the Lord. God may be testing us. What are a few good results from waiting on the Lord?

2. Matthew 18:23-35. Study this account of two debtors. What did the first one ask his master to do? Then what did that servant do? Do these stories apply to us? How?

3. Luke 8:15. What is necessary if one is to have a "good crop?" Does this principle of patience work in the lives of parents? Teachers? Ranchers? Students? How?

4. Romans 12:12. What are some ways that a person may go through tribulation? At such times, is patience needed? Share an experience where the two go together.

5. 2 Corinthians 12:12. The work of serving the Lord and seeing His hand of blessings upon the work demands what virtue? Why is patience needed in every work?

6. Hebrews 6:12. Why and how do you think that patience is involved with our eternal inheritance, or even with temporary blessings?

7. Hebrews 12:1. What kind of race are we running every day? Do those in athletic events show patience? How? Why is patience needed in every day living?

8. 1 Thessalonians 5:14. Do you find it difficult to be patient with family members as well as others outside the family circle? Can we be patient with everyone?

9. James 5:7. What great event of the future requires patience? How does a farmer teach a person patience?

10. James 5:11. What Old Testament man is a splendid example of patience? How can three or four "friends" like those in Job's circle "try" our faith? When? How?

Peace

—〰—

In 1519 Ponce de Leon of Spain first looked across the mountains of Panama and saw a great body of water. Hardly a breeze was blowing and the ocean looked like a sea of glass. He called that body of water the Pacific Ocean because of its peaceful condition at that time. He did not know that storms soon would explode across the water and the Pacific Ocean would be the opposite of anything calm and pacific. We want a peaceful life. God offers us the promise of peace in His Word, if we accept what is written.

1. Psalm 34:14. Do we search for health, wealth, and joy? This Scripture says that we should seek peace and pursue it. How do we seek peace? Is peace always possible?

2. Psalm 119:165. Define great peace? Would you like to have peace in church, home, and national life? Where can we find peace? What blessing comes from peace?

3. Isaiah 26:3. What does perfect peace mean? What does it mean to have the mind fixed on God? Where can this kind of utopian peace be demonstrated?

4. Isaiah 48:18, 22. If people hear and obey God's commands, what will be the result? According to verse 22, who does not have peace? Why is this true?

5. Luke 1:76-79. Who was the prophet who announced the coming of Jesus? What does Christ offer everyone? Why do we need to be guided in the path of peace?

6. John 14:27. What legacy did Christ promise His followers? What is the difference between Christ's peace and the peace of the world? Which is best? Why?

7. John 16:33. What teachings did Jesus share with His disciples? Why? In face of the tribulations that come, what should be our attitude? Why?

8. Romans 12:18. Why did Paul say that if it's possible to live peaceably with everyone? If it's possible, what can be done to improve changes with others?

9. Ephesians 2:14. Who is the real source of peace if a person is to have peace? Why do we believe this? What has Christ done to make living together easier?

10. Philippians 4:7. What takes place in the life of a person who trusts Christ as Savior? How great is God's peace? Why is it not possible to measure God's peace?

Pleasures

—ɯ—

A story has been told about a boy who walked up to a man and said, "I have a bird in my hand. Can you tell me if he is dead or alive?" The man waited a moment and answered, "That all depends. If I say he is dead you may turn him loose and show me that the bird is alive. If I say he is alive, you may crush the bird and he will be dead." What about pleasures? Are they right or wrong? That depends on how we handle them or what they are. The Bible shows that some pleasures are good and others are evil. Let's look again at what we can learn about pleasures from God's Word.

1. Psalm 36:7-9. This verse speaks of a river of God's pleasure. With His unfailing love, we find unending pleasure with God. Is this God's way or our own?

2. Psalm 111:2. Have we gazed at the moon and stars at night or looked at the sun by day? They are a part of God's works. How can we delight in God's creation?

3. Proverbs 21:17. This verse refers to evil pleasures, those that drag a person down. What are some evil pleasures that may drag a person down? Why?

4. Isaiah 44:28. Does God have eventual control of rulers and nations? Cyrus of Persia replaced the Babylonians. How did God touch the heart of Cyrus and why?

5. Isaiah 58:12-14. God promised a new day for Israel when they stopped doing their "own thing." What did they do, and what results did they see? What about today?

6. Ezekiel 18:23, 32. Does God want to chasten His people? Why or why not? Does He have pleasure in the death of the wicked? Why or why not?

7. Haggai 1:7-8, 12-14. What did God want His people to do? What promises did God make to them? How does God work with His people? Does God enjoy our success?

8. Luke 8:14. In the large context, where does the farmer sow his seed? What choked out the growth of some plants that came up? How does this truth apply today?

9. Luke 12:32. Why do some people in churches sometimes grow tired? Why did Jesus tell His followers not to be afraid? What does He promise us?

10. Revelation 4:11. God created the universe for His purpose and for His pleasure. Do you think that we will find pleasure in God's creation beyond the present life?

Poverty or poor

—ɷ—

In the book entitled *Encyclopedia of 7700 Illustrations*, Paul Lee Tan tells the story of David Brenner who came to the USA from his poverty-stricken background in Russia. In America, this sculptor soon became famous. He was the one who had engraved on the face of the penny the face of Abraham Lincoln who said that God must love the poor because He made so many of them. Nothing is inherently wrong in being poor or in being rich. The Bible says that God made both. Sometimes those who campaign most strongly to help the poor may speak only with words and not with their billfolds. Many who are wealthy give abundantly. Often times the poor share out of their poverty. Let's look at the topic of poverty.

1. Exodus 23:11; Deuteronomy 15:11. Land owners were told to let their land be idle every seventh year for what reason? Discuss this ancient rule. What's the lesson?

2. Psalm 102:17. What does God think of the poor and the destitute? Where are those people found? How does God respond to their prayers?

3. Proverbs 17:5; 19:17. How does God feel about those who mock the poor? If we help the poor, how do we lend to God? How does the Lord repay the lender?

4. Proverbs 20:13; 23:20-21; 28:19. Now the shoe is on "the other foot." What are the results of idleness, too much sleep, drinking and gluttony? Is everyone responsible?

5. Isaiah 3:15. Who is guilty of crushing the poor?" Why should we feel responsible to others? What about nations? What do those who talk about helping others do?

6. Amos 2:6-7. Who often became oppressors in the Old Testament? Does this happen today? Why or why not? What about economic sanctions?

7. Matthew 19:21. What did Jesus tell a rich man to do? What kind of treasures would a person have who gives away everything? Should everyone follow that route?

8. Romans 15:26-29. Since the Gentiles had benefited spiritually from the Israelites, what did Paul challenge the Gentiles to do? With whom can we share materially?

9. 2 Corinthians 6:10. What do you think of these words from Paul? Describe his sufferings. How did he make others rich? How can we follow His example?

10. 2 Corinthians 8:9. What was the status of Jesus before He came from heaven? How does He make others rich? How can we enrich the lives of others?

Praise

—⟋ⱴ⟍—

Praise in its many forms such as thanksgiving, gratitude, a-men, and other derivatives of the word appears more than 300 times in the Bible. How given to praising the Lord are we? If we read through the book of Psalms, we will be astounded at the dozens of time that the writers express praise to the Lord. Let's look at a few of the biblical references to praise in this sharing time.

1. Genesis 29:35. The fourth son of Jacob and Leah was named Judah, meaning "praise the Lord." Who came from Judah's tribe? How do we show Judah's good traits?

2. 1 Chronicles 23:5. At the dedication of Solomon's temple, how many people had the task of praising the Lord? Do you think we praise the Lord enough at worship times?

3. Psalm 71:8. Do you frequently fill your mouth with praises to the Lord? In what ways do we praise God? Think of the duration of our praise as this verse states.

4. Psalm 119:62, 164. David said he got up at midnight to praise the Lord. How many times a day did he praise the Lord? What experiences do we have of praise?

5. Psalms 148:1 to 150:6. Read, meditate, and comment on these three chapters of praise. Does about every thing praise the Lord? What about us?

6. Luke 1:62-64. Do you know about Zechariah and Elizabeth? What happened to that "old man?" Who was their son? What did people do when John was born?

7. Luke 19:28-40. What did people do in this story about Jesus? How did they praise the Lord? How did the Pharisees react? What did Jesus say?

8. Acts 3:1-8. What happened to a crippled man at the temple in Jerusalem? What did he do when he was healed? What should we do when Christ changes our lives?

9. Hebrews 13:15. What's the principal avenue of praise to the Lord? How long is our praise to go on? What do the words mean about "sacrifice of praise...with lips?"

10. Revelation 5:12-13 Who is the "Lamb" in this verse? Why is He worthy of praise? Who gives praise to the Lord in these verses? When can we praise Jesus?

Praying and prayers

—𝕞—

Before the battle of Edgehill in England, Sir John Astley lifted his hands toward Heaven and prayed, "Oh Lord, you know how busy I must be this day; if I forget you, do not forget me." Then he arose from his knees, and shouted to his troops, "March on, boys!"

God has a wonderful plan in operation that allows His people to speak to Him at any time. Praying is the privilege of all believers. The Bible teaches us about prayer.

1. Deuteronomy 9:9, 18, 25-29. How long was Moses on top of the mountain with the Lord? Why was he there and what did he ask God to do? Is long praying needed?

2. 1 Kings 18:36-39. Read the background story in verses 25-35. What did Elijah pray for and what was the result? What happens when we pray?

3. 2 Kings 19:19-20. Who threatened Israel? What did King Hezekiah and Isaiah ask God to do? What happened to Sennacherib? (Isaiah 37:36-38). Is prayer effective?

4. Psalm 55:16-17. What did God do when David called on Him in prayer? Should we have prayer times? When and where can we pray? Share a prayer experience.

5. Isaiah 59:1-4. Is God always capable and ready to rescue His people? Why does God sometimes refuse to hear prayers? What should we do for prayers to be heard?

6. Matthew 6:6-7. Why did Jesus emphasize the importance of secret praying? What does this Scripture teach about "vain repetitions?" What about public prayers?

7. Luke 22:41-44. Describe the prayer of Jesus in Gethsemane. What did Jesus say to His "inner circle?" Is it difficult to pray for God's will to be done? Why or why not?

8. John 15:7. How does Christ and His Word abide in us? What will Jesus do for His people who give Him full access to life? What does John 16:24 teach?

9. 1 Timothy 2:1-4. Who should we pray for? Why should we pray for each other and also for government leaders or rulers?

10. Revelation 5:8. Discuss this verse. What two items were in the bowls of the angels and elders? Do you have any prayers in heaven waiting to be answered?

Pride

—⁓—

One of Aesop's fables tells about a farmer's daughter who was taking a bucket of milk from the barn. She thought, "The money that I'll have after this milk is sold will buy 300 eggs. From these eggs, I can probably have 250 chickens. The chicks will grow fast so that by the end of the year when they're taken to the market, I can sell them and use the money to buy me a new dress. Then I will go to Christmas parties where young fellows will propose to me, but I will refuse everyone of them. At that moment, she tossed her head back with pride, the milk bucket fell to the ground, and all her imaginary schemes crashed, too. Pride causes the small and the great to fall. Let's take a close-up view of pride that attempts to place man in the center of his little world.

1. Exodus 18:11. Jethro learned about Pharaoh's defeat after he had mistreated God's people. What was the price he paid for pride? How does pride cost now?

2. Leviticus 26:18-21. If people stubbornly go on their way, how does God intervene? Are afflictions multiplied to the proud seven times? What should we learn?

3. 1 Samuel 2:3. Hannah rejoiced over the birth of her son. Samuel gave her "righteous pride," but not arrogance. How did she give glory to God? Can we do the same?

4.   Proverbs 16:5, 18. What attitudes do some people have before their fall? How does Genesis 11:1-9 illustrate the danger of pride? How can we be careful?

5.   Ezekiel 30:6. The prophet Ezekiel wrote about some of the allies of Egypt. Why did that nation's strength fail? What happens to allies when we exclude God from life?

6.   Jeremiah 13:15-19. What warning did Israel receive if they refused God's message? What was Jeremiah's response? How do we feel when people turn away from God?

7.   Daniel 4:28-37. What did Nebuchadnezzar say about Babylon? What happened to him? What did he say after God restored him? What can we learn from that king?

8.   Luke 18:10-14. What kind of a prayer did the religious pharisee have? Do we sometimes let God know how important we are? Why is some praying ineffective?

9.   James 4:6. Why does God oppose prayer that is filled with pride? In contrast, what does God give to the humble?

10. 1 John 2:16. Why does the Bible tell us not to "love the world?" What do the words about "the pride of life" mean? What does 1 Peter 5:6 say about humility?

Prisons and inmates

—w—

In the years 2006, the United States of America has in state and federal prisons more than 150,000 prisoners. The vast majority are inmates in those institutions because of breaking the law and various kinds of crimes against others. Our prison system provides beds, meals, and entertainment for those behind bars. A few are so pleased with their treatment that they would rather stay in prison than be set free. However, prison life is not ideal. The Bible challenges us to minister to those in prison. Let's look at this topic.

1. Genesis 39:6-20. Joseph went to prison in Egypt because Potiphar's wife falsely accused him. How can people live pure lives in face of all the temptations they face?

2. Judges 16:21, 25. Who was Samson? What was the secret of his strength? How did he lose it? What tragedy happened to him? How do some flirt with sin?

3. Jeremiah 37:21; 38:6-13. Who was Jeremiah? Why was he sent to prison? Who saved him from death? Are many of God's servants in prison today?

4. Matthew 11:2; 14:6-12. Why was John the Baptist in prison? What happened to him? What did Jesus say about him? Do Christ's followers always prosper?

5.   Matthew 25-34-40. What kind of ministry we have today? What blessing is promised to Christians who don't limit their ministry to "church going?"

6.   Luke 4:18-19. Where was Jesus when He announced the kind of ministry He had come to do? Are we following in His steps? Can we describe service to Christ?

7.   Luke 22:31-33. How did Simon Peter express his commitment to Christ? Do we sometimes say what we are not ready to do at that moment?

8.   Acts 16:22-34. Why were Paul and Silas in prison? What were they doing at midnight? What did they do after the "jail house rock?" Are we witnessing?

9.   Ephesians 4:1. Paul was a prisoner in Caesarea for two years before his Roman jail time (Acts 24:27). What did he do in Rome? How can we serve God where we are?

10. 2 Timothy 1:8. Paul's first jail time in Rome was 61-63 A.D. His last incarceration was 67 A.D. What did he write to Timothy? How does the text apply to us?

Promises

—ᨦᨩ—

When a child does not behave, that one may say to his mother or dad, "Don't spank me this time, and I'll never do that again." When people feel the pressures of life coming down on them, they may be ready to make just about any kind of promise. We also like to hear promises, such as, "You're going to have a great birthday present or Christmas present." Adults like to hear about promises such as job promotions, a longer vacation, or a salary increase. We find a lot of promises in the Bible that have eternal importance. Look at a few of them.

1. Genesis 28:20. What did Jacob expect God to do for him? What promises did he make to God? What are some practical promises that we should make to God?

2. Deuteronomy 9:25-29. What did Moses tell God people that would say if He didn't keep His promise about taking Israel into the Promised Land?

3. 1 Kings 8:56. Why did Solomon praise the Lord? Did any promise that God made to Moses fail? Can you find any of those promises of God in the book of Exodus?

4. Zephaniah 3:17. This verse gives some fulfilled promises. God is with His people. He saves, takes delight in His people, and rejoices over us. Discuss these ideas.

5. Luke 6:38-39. What blessing comes to those who do not judge or condemn others? What promise is implied in this text to those who forgive and to those who share?

6. Acts 2:29-33. What promise did God give to David? Who already sits on David's throne? What does it mean to have Jesus on the throne of your life?

7. Acts 2:36-39. When the Jews heard Peter say that the crucified Christ was Lord, what did they ask? What did Peter tell them to do? What gift would they receive?

8. Romans 4:20-22. What response did Abraham have to God's promise to give him a son? Why was that a test for Abraham? Why should we believe God's promises?

9. Ephesians 6:1-3. What is the first commandment with promise? Do parents have anything to do with the fulfilling of that promise of a longer life? How?

10. 2 Peter 1:4. By the Lord's power, He gives us life and godliness. What are some of the precious promises that the Lord also offers us? What benefit are they?

Questions

—◊—

S mall children sometimes ask their parents a hundred questions
a day! Some may ask that many questions every ten minutes.
They may say, "why," "when," "how," and other questions. Numbers
of questions are in the Bible. Let's look at a few Bible questions,
answer them, and apply the lessons to our lives.

1. Genesis 3:9. Why and how did Adam and Eve try to hide from
    God? What happens if we try to run from God? Does disobedi-
    ence to God frighten anyone? Why?

2. Deuteronomy 1:12. Who had heavy burdens and why? What
    can parents, teachers, and most everyone do to keep from
    getting overloaded with responsibilities?

3. Isaiah 6:11. What did God want Isaiah to do? For how long?
    Does God want us to witness? What are some ways to witness?
    Tell about a witnessing experience.

4. Jeremiah 2:36. Are we consistent in the way we live? Why do
    some people "flip flop" and change their ways? Why are we
    disobedient to God?

5. Malachi 3:8. Can people steal from God? What are some ways
    in which anyone can cheat on God?

6. Matthew 7:23. Why do we look at a little stuff in our neighbor's eyes and overlook the evil that's in our own eyes? How is this wrong happening today?

7. Matthew 18:21. Has anyone ever done anything against you? How do you feel about "being hurt?" What should our reaction be toward those who wrong us?

8. Romans 14:10. Why is it easy to criticize? Do we love the chance to put others down? What can we do instead of being judgmental?

9. 1 Corinthians 6:7-8. Should Christians go to court against fellow believers? Why or why not? How should we solve our problems?

10. James 4:14. How does James describe the length of life? See Psalm 90:10, 12. Who or what should guide our decisions?

Reconciliation

—ɯ—

One of the many heart-touching stories in Genesis relates to Joseph and his brothers. Briefly, they sold Joseph into slavery. About 13 years later when the brothers made a trip to Egypt, looking for food, they confronted Joseph. Soon Joseph let them know who he was. He embraced them and wept profusely. The years of broken relationships became restored because Joseph took the step necessary to bring about reconciliation.

Most people need to be reconciled to God as well as to one another. God makes restoration possible with Himself and with others through the gift of Jesus, His only Son. The offended Lord removes all hindrances from a broken relationship, but each person has a part to play. We must accept the forgiveness which God offers. Reconciliation between Jew and Gentile, between family members, and between nations can take place if we go God's way. Will we do it?

1. Genesis 27:41; chs. 32-33. Chapter 27 tells the story of a broken relationship between Jacob and Esau. Did they ever become fully reconciled? Why not?

2. Matthew 5:23-24. If two believers have a conflict, they should not bring an offering to God without first settling their differences. How would this effect churches?

3. 1 Corinthians 7:11. Paul says separated couples should seek reconciliation. Whether divorced or not, reconciliation is needed. What does this imply?

4. Romans 5:10-11; 11:15. Even while some are enemies of God, how can they be reconciled? What blessings come through restored relationships?

5. 2 Corinthians 5:18-20. Who initiates and makes possible reconciliation with God? What work should the reconciled do? Why is there an urgency in this work?

6. Ephesians 2:16-18. What has Jesus done for Jews and Gentiles? How does reconciliation between people take place? What does God do for the reconciled?

7. Philippians 4:2-3. Who were Euodia and Syntche? What appeal did Paul make to them? What would restored relationships between Christians bring about today?

8. Colossians 1:19-22. What kind of personal relationships would take place if Christians accepted God's reconciliation? What would happen to hostility?

9. 2 Timothy 4:11. What problem erupted between Paul and Mark? (Acts 15:36-41). During Paul's last imprisonment, what did he ask Timothy to do? Why? Apply.

10. Philemon 1:8-19. Who was Philemon and who was Onesimus? What happened between the two? How did Paul get involved? How does this story apply to us?

Redemption

—⋙—

S everal years ago an Exxon oil executive was captured by some guerilla fighters in Cordoba, Argentina. The "montoneros" demanded something like five million dollars for the man's release, If my memory has not mudded the story, it seems that the company paid the ransom or redemption price for him.

On another level, Jesus came to pay a heavy price for mankind's redemption from Satan. Theologians have debated quite often about our redemption from Satan. We do know that Jesus, the Redeemer, came and on the cross paid the price for our release. Let's let the Scripture explain some facts about our spiritual and physical redemption.

1. Genesis 3:15. Who brought about man's enslavement to sin? Did "we" cooperate with the devil in our bondage to sin? Who crushed the devil's head and how?

2. Job 19:25-27. What positive statement did Job give about the Redeemer? In what way did the Job describe his future relationship with Jesus?

3. Psalm 130:7. Why should Israel's or God's people place their hope in God? What will God do for His people? What do you think about God's goodness to you?

4. Isaiah 51:11. Are the ransomed of the Lord going to return with joy and singing to Him? Why? What does it mean for sorrows and sighing to flee away?

5. Romans 3:23-24. Why do people need God's redemption? What does it mean that everyone sins? How is mankind made right with God? Who provides redemption?

6. Galatians 3:11. Does the Law save? How did Christ redeem us from the Law's curse? How do the blessings promised to Abraham and Israel come to Christians?

7. Hebrews 9:22, 25-28; 10:11-14. Through whom is mankind redeemed? How did Christ pay for man's sin? How many times did Christ die for our sins?

8. 1 Peter 1:18-21. What happens to those who want to buy their salvation? How are we saved? When did God choose us? What happened to Christ after His death?

9. Titus 2:10-14. How does redemption come to us? What should be the Christian's concern today? Are we eager to do what is good?

10. Revelation 5:9. Why was Christ worthy to take the scroll from an angel's hand? Who has been purchased from sin by Christ's blood? What future do we have?

Repent or repentance

—w—

Years ago Dr. Conner stated in a class at Southwestern Seminary in Fort Worth that repentance means a "change of mind." One student said, "Dr. Conner, that definition sounds too simple. Doesn't repentance mean more than that?" The professor asked, "Young man, are you married?" The student said "No sir." Dr. Conner then said, "I didn't think you were because if you were married you would know that when a wife says she has "changed her mind" that a total revolution takes place. The Greek word repent is "metanoia." It means to change radically one's opinion, to go in an opposite direction.

1. Genesis 6:6 Repentance in this text indicates that God was grieved over man's sin. When man repents, God has a new attitude and pardons him. (Numbers 23:19).

2. 1 Kings 8:46-51. Solomon prayed at the temple dedication. If Israel sinned and enemies captured them, what hope did they have? How can we be forgiven?

3. Job 42:6. Job admitted that he had said things without understanding. When Job "saw the Lord," what did he do? What should we do when we have a vision of God?

4. Jeremiah 8:4-11. Man oftentimes is like a horse charging into battle. He does not turn and repent. How do these verses describe ancient Israel and us?

5. Ezekiel 14:6; 18:30, 32. God's prophets called for His people to turn from idolatry and stop their detestable practices. Should we "stop our meanness" and change?

6. Joel 2:12-14. We need to return to God with fasting, weeping, and mourning. God is slow to anger, gracious, and gives blessings to the repentant. What's our reaction?

7. Matthew 3:4-10. How did John the Baptist describe repentance? Why did he say everyone should repent? What are some areas in life where repentance is needed?

8. Acts 5:29-33. What message did Simon Peter preach? What did Jesus do for our benefit? How did some respond to the message? What should we do?

9. Acts 17:30. Read carefully Paul's message that he preached at Mars Hill in Athens, Greece. What did he say that God commanded? What sins call for our repentance?

10. Hebrews 12:17. Read Genesis 27:1-38. What happened in Esau's life? Why didn't repentance help him? When does repentance come too late?

Rest

—⚏—

One story tells about a lady who had inscribed on her tombstone words that bring a smile to all of us. The words are: "Here lies an old woman who was always tired, She lived in a house where help was not hired; Her last words were, 'Dear friend I am going, Where cooking ain't done nor mopping nor sewing; But everything there is exact to my wishes, For where they don't eat, there's no washing of dishes. Don't mourn for me, Don't mourn for me never! I'm going to do nothing forever and ever'!"

Sometimes we want rest from the burdens and responsibilities of life. The Bible gives hope to all who long for rest.

1. Genesis 2:2-3. When God finished His creative work, He rested. God was not tired, but He contemplated and enjoyed all of it. How can we enjoy our work??

2. Genesis 18:4. Abraham saw three "men" at his door. He rushed to wash their feet, give them rest, and food. He wanted to see them refreshed. Do we need refreshing?

3. Exodus 23:10-12. After six days of work, man needed rest. His servants and animals did, too. Even the land needs rest after six years of production. What of us?

4. 2 Chronicles 14:1-6. King Asa of Judah tore down idols, and led his people to honor God. No wars broke out during his rule. Do we need this kind of rest today?

5. Psalm 55:6. David wanted to "fly away" like a bird and be at rest. What are some burdens that make us want to fly away? What kind of rest do we want?

6. Psalm 132:14. God chose Zion as His dwelling place. How does God find in us His resting place? When God finds His home in us, what does He do for us?

7. Isaiah 28:12. God offered a resting place for His people. They did not listen to God. They became ensnared by their enemies. What happens to us when we disobey?

8. Jeremiah 6:16. What ancient paths did God want His people to follow? What was their former way of life? What blessing comes to those who live in God's ways?

9. Matthew 11:28-29. What invitation does Christ give to those who are weary? Why do we get in this condition? What does "rest for your souls" mean?

10. Hebrews 4:3, 9-11. Since we believe in the Lord, what should be our heritage, our blessing now? How can we labor to enter God's rest? Why should we not fear?

Rewards

—w—

A braham Lincoln borrowed a book from a neighbor farmer on the life of George Washington. One rainy night he sat up reading the book, but put it down in what he thought was a safe place in the family's log cabin. The next morning Lincoln found the book soaked with water. He took it back to the owner and offered to work in the man's corn field for three days to pay for the book because he didn't have any money. When the work in the field had been done, the man gave Lincoln the book as a reward for his work. Most everyone has interest in rewards of whatever kind they may be. The Bible meets us at this level of our interest and has encouraging words for anyone in God's service.

1. Genesis 15:1. When Abraham responded to God and left his home south of Babylon, God rewarded him. Why didn't he have to be afraid? What was his reward?

2. 2 Chronicles 15:7-8. What was good King Asa told to do? How did Asa feel about the challenge? How did the Lord reward him? How does God reward us for work?

3. Psalms 103:2. What does God do with our sins? Why doesn't God reward us according to our sin? How do you feel about this kind of "no reward?"

4.   Proverbs 11:18. If we want a sure reward, what must we do? How can we sow righteousness? Where can righteousness be sown? What kind of sower are you??

5.   Proverbs 25:22. How do we treat our enemies? What will God do for those who give food and water to enemies? What would happen if nations practiced this principle?

6.   Matthew 5:10-12. How would you react if you were persecuted and hated because of your faith? How should we react? Who rewards the persecuted? How? When?

7.   Matthew 10:40-42. What's the reward of a true prophet? Can others receive his reward? How? What can be done for those who are thirsty? What promise is here?

8.   1 Corinthians 3:5-8. What does it mean to plant and water in God's kingdom? Who has done this? Who can do this work? What reward does God offer?

9.   1 Corinthians 9:17. Do we sometimes work because we "have to?" When and where does work never stop? If we willingly work, what is the advantage?

10. Colossians 3:24. How can we let our work in any circumstance be done as unto the Lord? What inheritance will God give people who work for His honor?

Riches

—〰—

The most wealthy person in all history and eternity is God. The Bible states that the silver and gold belong in God's portfolio. The cattle on a thousand hills belong to God. The Lord of the universe lets man have possession of "things" for a while, but eventually everything falls back into God's corner. When we talk about riches, we can't say that wealth is good or evil within itself. The way we deal with riches determines its status. Numbers of rich people are righteous and many poor people may be evil. The reverse is also true. Look at some cases of wealthy people in the Scriptures.

1. Genesis 13:1-2. When God called Abraham from Chaldea, he was wealthy. He later came from Egypt with "cattle, silver and gold." What kind of man was he?

2. Psalm 49:16-20. If a billionaire came to talk to you, how would you feel? What do rich people take with them when they die? What quality do rich and poor need?

3. Proverbs 10:4. What do those who refuse to work accumulate? What kind of disposition must a person have who wants to gain wealth? Is that an easy route?

4. Proverbs 18:11. Can wealth be like a strong tower or like a fortified city? Why or why not? Can poverty be a cure for the ills of life? Who or what is our hope?

5. Proverbs 27:24. How long does a rich person have his wealth? What can cause the collapse of riches? What does Proverbs 23:4 teach about gaining wealth?

6. Jeremiah 9:23-24. What temptation does a person with wealth face? How do the poor often feel? Jealousy? Envy? In what should we "boast?"

7. Matthew 19:23-24. Why did Jesus say that it is hard for a rich person to enter heaven? What of Abraham, Job, and Barnabas (Acts 4:31)? What of anyone?

8. Matthew 27:57. Joseph of Arimathea witnessed the crucifixion of Christ. He had become Christ's disciple. How did he show his faith? How do we prove our faith?

9. Luke 19:1-10. Why did Zaccheus tell Jesus that he was ready to restore four-fold anything he had taken from others? Why did Jesus go home with Zaccheus?

10. Revelation 2:9. What classification did the church at Smyrna receive from Jesus? How was that poor church also rich? How can our church be rich?

Roots

—ᴍ—

A lot of "root plowing" takes place in Texas where mesquite and cactus grow. Ranchers and farmers continually "root out" the plants or trees that have no value so that cotton and grain can be productive. When I grew up on a farm we seemed to be always digging up the roots of persimmon and sassafras bushes, as well as crab grass, so that the land would be more productive. Of course, we want roots on anything that is valuable to continually grow in order that productivity can take place. The Bible has volumes of truth about the root system whether in people, animal, or plant life.

1. Deuteronomy 29, 18, 28. God warned His people not to turn away from Him and allow roots of idolatry and bitterness to grow. Why is this warning needed today?

2. Proverbs 12:12. God says righteous roots flourish. What does this mean? What can be done to keep the good roots growing? When and where should the righteous grow?

3. Isaiah 53:2. To what or to whom does the "root out of Jesse" refer? Why is this "root" said to come out of a "dry ground?" Elaborate on Isaiah 11:1-2, 10.

4. Matthew 3:10. Why did John the Baptist say the ax was chopping away at the root of the tree? Do you think God will also root out those who are false in His kingdom?

5. Matthew 13:6. A sower let some seed fall on stony ground? What happened to the seed? Why did it wither? Are those who "wither" God's people? Why or why not?

6. Matthew 13:29. Do you believe that tares come up among the wheat today? Why is it dangerous to try to "root out" the tares? Who can handle the tares? When?

7. Romans 11:16-18. Paul wrote that if the root is holy the tree will also be holy. Why did some of the branches get broken off? Who gets grafted in? Spend time here.

8. Ephesians 3:17. If Christ is in the heart and we are rooted in Him, what takes place in the life of believers? What advantage do we have because of this "root system?

9. Hebrews 12:15. What kind of root can spring up in life? What will bitterness cause? What is bitterness? How does bitterness defile or contaminate others?

10. Jude 1:11-13. What happens to those who seem to be in God's kingdom, but who go the way of Cain and Korah? Who are false shepherds? What happens to those roots?

Salvation

—ᵐᵐ—

When an accident happens on a highway, we may say that the "jaws-of-life" rescued the survivors. When a person is pulled out of a burning building, some will say that the fire fighters saved that one. A person who is drowning may be pulled out of a lake or river. We may say that the life guards saved that person.

Salvation is a common word that is used in many circumstances. When the Bible refers to salvation we normally think of a person who is saved through his or her faith in Christ. A shocking fact is that salvation appears more often in the Old Testament than in the New Testament. About 120 times the word salvation appears in the Old Testament. The New Testament uses the word about 40 times. God is involved in our salvation. Let's view a few verses that mention this truth of being saved.

1. Exodus 14:13. When Moses had prepared to lead the Israelites from their bondage in Egypt, the Lord asked them to stand still and see His salvation. What did God do?

2. 2 Chronicles 20:15-17. King Jehoshaphat of Israel faced enemies. A prophet told him for his army to take their position and watch God work. Describe the scenario.

3. Psalm 27:1-3. The Psalms mention God's salvation more than any other book. How did David describe God? Why did he not have to be afraid? Why aren't we afraid?

4. Psalms 68:19-20. Why should we be praising God? What can He do for those who trust Him? What does it mean that God saves us from death?

5. Isaiah 12:2. This chapter from Isaiah emphasizes God as the one who gives salvation. What other blessings does God offer? Do you now have His salvation?

6. Isaiah 25:9. When we trust the Lord, the Bible declares that He saves us. With His salvation, what should we do? What does it mean to rejoice and be glad?

7. Matthew 1:21-23. Who was the earthly mother of Jesus? Is Mary the "Mother of God?" Why not? Why did God send Jesus? What does Emmanuel mean?

8. Acts 4:12. What does this verse state about salvation? Can another person save? Does "no other name under heaven" exclude everyone except Jesus?

9. Romans 1:16. Can you define the gospel? What did Jesus do? The resurrected Christ is God's power to do what? What is a person saved from? How is a person saved?

10. Ephesians 2:8-9. God's grace means His kindness that no one deserves. Does a person have to believe? How is this a gift? Can we boast of earning salvation?

Satan or the devil

—∿—

B ank robbers and others who want to deceive people often have an "alias" or an assumed name. The devil has various names such as dragon, serpent, the father of lies, and deceiver. Satan is the world's greatest counterfeit or pretender. Look at a few of the actions of the one who once was the chief of God's good angels.

1. Genesis 3:1-15. How did the devil become involved in the Fall of mankind? What did God tell the devil that would eventually happen to Him? What was the event?

2. Job 1:6-12, 21. What are a few of the devil's habits? Why do you think that Satan attacks God's character? In what ways can the evil one attack God's people today?

3. Zechariah 3:1-5. What did Satan do against Joshua, God's high priest? (This Joshua was not the helper of Moses). What do you think Satan likes to do today?

4. Matthew 4:1-11. Discuss how the devil tempted Jesus? How did Jesus rebuff those temptations? How can we survive the devil's attacks?

5. Luke 22:31-34. Why did Jesus warn Peter of Satan's attacks? Why do we need to heed warnings about Satanic attacks? What is our hope when Satan tempts us?

6. John 8:44. In what ways did Jesus describe Satan? Do you think our enemy ever lets up on us? If a person does not belong to Jesus, who controls him or her?

7. 2 Corinthians 4:3-4. Who is the devil called in this verse? What is one of Satan's works? Why do you think the devil is successful in his world-wide work?

8. 1 Peter 5:8. Discuss some of a lion's habits? Why are lions dangerous? How does Satan act like a lion? How does God protect His people from the devil?

9. 1 John 3:8-10. What is one reason that Jesus came to this world? How are God's children and the devil's followers distinguished? Can we always identify them?

10. Revelation 20:1-3, 10. What is the final destiny of the devil? Do you think the Bible lets us know enough about Satan? Why or why not?

Scripture or the Bible

—w—

Charles Spurgeon of England said, "You don't have to defend the Bible. It is like a tiger. Turn it loose and it will defend itself." We don't need to have battles over God's Book. Our commission is to learn and proclaim its truths. The word *Bible* means *book*. Our Bible is made up of two sections, the Old Testament and the New Testament. The first part of the Bible has 39 books; the New Testament has 27. Let's notice some very important truths about the Bible.

1. Joshua 1:9. Where should God's Word be? When and how do we meditate on His Word? What happens to those who do what this Scripture says?

2. Job 23:12. Most people eat three meals a day. Job said that he recognized God's Word as more important than the food he ate each day. What about us?

3. Psalm 119:11, 105, 130. Let's discover what God's Word can do for us. It keeps us from sin, is a light for our path, and gives understanding. Can any other book do this?

4. Isaiah 40:8. Most books have a short shelf life. Grass dies soon. Flowers fade and lose their beauty. What did Isaiah say about God's Word? Is this a proven fact?

5. Jeremiah 15:16; 23:29. What happened when Jeremiah ate God's Word? What comparison did he make of God's Word? How is the Bible like a rock and hammer?

6. John 20:31. Jesus did incredible work and taught eternal lessons during His ministry. What is the major reason why John wrote his gospel? What does Christ offer us?

7. Colossians 3:16. What does it mean to have God's Word "dwelling in us?" What does "richly" mean? In what ways does God's Book cause a reaction in us?

8. 2 Timothy 3:16. What does this verse specifically teach about inspiration? In what ways is the Bible beneficial to us? What do verses 15 and 17 also teach?

9. Hebrews 4:12. In contrast to a dead book, what about the Bible? How is the "sharpness" of the Bible described? What analysis does it make of one's life?

10. 2 Peter 1:21. How did the Old Testament prophets speak God's message? In what ways did the Holy Spirit effect their proclamation?

Shepherds and sheep

—⟰—

Goat and sheep ranches are common in many countries of the world. We know a lot about sheep, but don't hear too much of shepherds. The Bible, however, is a source book about shepherds and sheep. We can learn about ourselves, God's people, and Jesus as we look at references to shepherds and sheep.

1. 1 Samuel 17:34-36. David said that a lion and bear had attacked his sheep one time. He rescued the sheep from the lion and the bear. How can we care for God's sheep?

2. Psalm 23:1-6. Who is our true shepherd? In what ways does He care for us? What do the words "not want" mean? How does the Lord remove fear from us?

3. Isaiah 40:11. How does God take care of His flock? How does He lead the young? What does God say to the under-shepherds or leaders of His people?

4. Ezekiel 34:1-6. Rather than caring for their sheep, what is the shepherds main interest? What do they do for the weak and straying? How do they rule the sheep?

5. Luke 2:10. On the night when Christ was born in Bethlehem, what were some shepherds doing? Was their work convenient? Is it easy to watch over "sheep?"

6. Luke 15:4-5. When a shepherd noticed one missing sheep, what did he do? What attitude did he have when he found his sheep? How should we react at such times?

7. John 10:14. Who is our Good Shepherd? Do his sheep know Him? Does He know them? What did the Good Shepherd do for His sheep? What's the message for us?

8. John 21:15-17. What question did Jesus ask Simon Peter? What did Jesus tell Peter to do for His lambs and sheep? How do we care for God's people?

9. 1 Peter 2:25. What are many of God's people doing? When they return to the Shepherd, how are they received? Why?

10. 1 Peter 5:1-4. How may "pastors" best take care of God's people? Who is their owner? How can leaders serve willingly without being bosses and demagogues?

Sin

—∿∿—

People who want to know if they are experts at shooting sometimes put up a target or mark and try to hit the "bull's eye." If
the bullet goes within a small spot within the center of the target,
they reach their goal.

Sin means that a person has missed his or her goal of rightness.
Sin in Greek is pronounced "ha-mar-tia." The Bible uses the word
sin many times to indicate a person's failure. Other words such as
transgressions, faults, iniquities, evil, etc. also indicate that we fail
to do right. Let's view sin in ten different settings from the Bible.

1. Genesis 4:7. Why did Cain kill Abel? What did God say to
    Cain? What did he say to God? What was the result of Cain's
    dastardly deed?

2. Genesis 39:9. Who was Joseph and what temptation did he
    face? How did he avoid the sin? Joseph said that the sin would
    be against what person? Why?

3. Numbers 32:23. What did two and one half tribes of Israel want
    to do when their land had been conquered? What did Joshua
    say to them? How is sin revealed?

4. Deuteronomy 24:16. When fathers sin, who is responsible? When children sin, who must take the blame? Is everyone responsible for himself? Why or why not?

5. Proverbs 21:4. Why do you think that "the plowing of the wicked" is sin in God's sight? Does this mean that the daily work of non-believers is wrong? Why?

6. Ecclesiastes 9:18. What can one sinner do? What are some good things that can be destroyed by one person? How do we deal with the "one sinner?"

7. Isaiah 1:18. What's the hope of a person who sins? Why does God offer cleansing for nations and individuals? What is a forgiven person compared to?

8. Romans 3:23; 6:23. Who sins? What happens when a person sins? What's the result of sin? In contrast to death because of sin, what does God offer? What is a gift?

9. Luke 15:18, 21. What or who is a prodigal? In the parable of Jesus, where did the son go and what did he do? What did his father say when his son returned?

10. 1 John 1:9. Who does "we" in this verse include? What should we do when we sin? What does God do when confession is made? How many sins are forgiven?

Singing and songs

—ɯ—

A Jewish legend says that after God created the universe that He called His angels and asked them their opinion of what He had made. One said, "One more thing is needed, and that is the sound of praise to the Creator." Then God moved, according to legend, and created music whose sound was echoed in the wind, in the song of birds, and in the music of people's voices.

As we sing hymns of praise to the Lord, we should remember who God is, that He is not deaf, and that the message should be one that God's people can understand. Most people do not have hearing problems and don't need to have them in later life because of music that sometimes can almost burst the eardrums. Paul wrote, "If a trumpet gives an uncertain sound, who can prepare himself for war?" Consider some Bible references about music and song.

1. Exodus 15:1-18. Moses and Israel sang a long song to God. What does this chapter teach us about God, His enemies, and His people. Do hymns instruct us?

2. Psalm 104:33. An assignment for this week is to memorize this verse. How long should we sing to the Lord? Have you praised God in song today? Why not?

3. Psalm 137:1-6. What did the Babylonians ask the Israelites or Jews to do? What was their response? Can we, or do we, sing to the Lord in difficult places?

4. Psalm 145:1-7. According to this Psalm, what are some reasons for singing to the Lord? What does it mean to joyfully sing of God's righteousness?

5. Isaiah 35:1-10. Who should be helped by us? How does the prophet describe our pilgrimage to Zion or to heaven? How should our pilgrimage end? Will it?

6. Isaiah 44:21-23. Who are God's people? Does He have two groups? What is God doing for us? What two great reasons are given for singing to the Lord?

7. Zephaniah 3:17. How does God feel about His people? What do you think about God singing over you? Have you ever listened to one of His solos just for you?

8. Matthew 26:30. What does this verse say happened at the close of the "Last Supper?" Where were the disciples and where did they go after a hymn?

9. Ephesians 5:19. Can we communicate by singing? Are our songs spiritual? Is the message understood? Does our singing glorify the Lord? In what ways?

10. Revelation 15:3. The song of Moses and the Lamb that is sung in heaven tells what about Moses and God's people? What does the "song of the Lamb" mean?

Sleep

—〰—

Everyone sleeps. A new-born baby may sleep 18 to 20 hours a day. Senior citizens sometimes sleep long hours. The dictionary defines sleep as a state of torpid inactivity. One may find negative and positive results of sleeping. The Bible gives many examples of those who sleep. Consider the following references to sleep.

1. Genesis 2:21. Why did God cause Adam to fall into a "deep sleep?" What reaction do you think Adam had when he awakened?

2. Genesis 28:10-16. Who was Jacob? Why did he leave home? Do you think he slept very well, using a rock for a pillow? What happened to Jacob while he slept?

3. Judges 16:19. Who was Samson and what was the secret of his strength? How did he lose his strength? How do people lose their strength today?

4. Psalms 121:1-8. What person never goes to sleep? While we sleep, what benefits can the Lord give us? Do you ever thank God that He stays awake for your welfare?

5. Proverbs 6:4-11. What does Solomon say a person should do who sleeps too much? What creature teaches us to stay awake? What danger befalls a sluggard?

6. Jonah 1:6. Who was God's prophet who fell asleep? Where was he, and why did he go to sleep? What reactions do we have when we shirk responsibilities?

7. Matthew 13:25. What happens to those who sleep when they should be awake? Who is an enemy that can cause damage in God's cause when His servants sleep? How?

8. Luke 9:32. When Christ went to Gethsemane to pray, where did He leave His disciples? What happened to them? How and when do we face that risk?

9. Acts 12:6. Where was Simon Peter and what was he doing in Jerusalem when he was fastened to some guards? Did he have a restless night? How would you have felt?

10. Romans 13:11 Paul wrote about being awake spiritually. Why should we stay awake? How do many sleep spiritually? Why is such a life dangerous?

Strife or conflicts

—⚍—

If you ever pass by a school and the children and youth are outside, most seem to be having a great time. However, one or two of that bunch may not be getting along too well together. Sometimes even fights break out between them. Troubles explode when two teams play against one another. Don't go to a tavern or bar to watch what goes on, but amidst all the frolicking and laughter, sometimes a fight will erupt during that "happy hour." Troubles are universal, aren't they? Let's see what we can learn about strife or conflicts from a few examples in the Bible.

1. Genesis 13:8. What problem did Abraham and Lot's workers have? What solution did Abraham offer? What's the godly way to handle problems?

2. Proverbs 10:12. What is one source of strife? Where can quarrels happen? What's the solution to problems according to this verse? What is your reaction?

3. Proverbs 17:1. Notice a contrast in this verse. Do you prefer a banquet table with "nit picking" or a simple diet with peace? Why? How do you have your choice?

4. Proverbs 17:9. What happens to a person who becomes offended through disputes? Is it easy to conquer a fortress or fortified city? What about an offended person?

5. Proverbs 20:3. Why is it an honor to avoid strife? Do you follow the "high road" of peace or the "low road" of disputings? How can you help the "low road" group?

6. Proverbs 28:25. What is one sure source of dissention and unending troubles? What is the contrast to stirring up problems? Should we help those who "fume and fuss?"

7. Proverbs 30:33. Have you heard grandparents talk about "churning milk?" What happens if we "twist noses?" When and how is strife caused and settled?

8. Luke 22:24. A dispute broke out among the disciples about which one was the greatest? When did that happen? What did Jesus say? What do you say?

9. Philippians 2:3-4. Paul gave counsel to the Philippians about being unselfish and esteeming others better than themselves. How do we practice this attitude today?

10. James 3:13-16. Read carefully these verses. What choices does a person have when faced with possible contentions? What is the source of problems? Do you agree?

Suffering and pain

—ᲚᲚᲔ—

One of the great men in Old Testament times was Job. He lost his family, possessions, and at last his health. Do good people suffer? If we're totally committed to Christ, will this assure us of health and prosperity? Let's look at what the Scriptures teach.

1. Jeremiah 20:1. God called Jeremiah to be one of his prophets (1:2). However, that prophet suffered beatings and imprisonment (Hebrews 11:36-38). What about today?

2. Matthew 16:21. Jesus told His disciples that He faced in Jerusalem a severe trial of rejection and suffering and death. If the world killed Jesus, what can we expect?

3. Acts 5:40-41. When the Apostles of Jesus met flogging and rejection soon after Pentecost, what was their reaction? How do you think you would have reacted?

4. Acts 9:16. When the Lord saved Paul on the road to Damascus (or about that time) he also heard something of the ill treatment and suffering he would face. What of us?

5. Romans 8:17-18. The future of God's people is one of glory. What does the Bible tell may happen to the followers of Jesus before their glory? Is suffering worth it?

6. 2 Corinthians 12:7-12. Why did Paul have to endure sufferings? What did he pray? What promise did he receive? What was his attitude toward suffering?

7. Philippians 1:29. What decision can any person make when that one faces Jesus? What may believers expect on the "negative" side? Who do we suffer for?

8. Hebrews 5:7-8. What kind of experiences in suffering did Jesus experience? What did he learn from His sufferings? What can we learn from suffering?

9. Jude 1:7. What kind of punishment can evil doers expect? Jude's reference is about what cities and what sins? Will God punish wicked people who refuse to change?

10. Revelation 2:10. The church at Smyrna (and any church) faces suffering? For how long? What blessing comes to those who endure? How does Satan want to ruin us?

Tears

—〜〜—

At one time or another most everyone cries. A wedding may bring a flood of tears to the bride and the parents of both the bride and groom. When death occurs people often suffer tears of sorrow. When a person has a reward for some outstanding work, tears of rejoicing may begin to flow. When a team wins a game, many people "jump up and down" in celebration, and at such a time some shed tears. Babies cry, young people may weep, and adults know about tears. Think about this word "tears."

1. 1 Kings 20:5. What did King Hezekiah do when he was told that he would die? What prophet prayed for him? Isaiah 38:5. How is prayer effective?

2. Esther 8:3. Who was Esther? Who was Haman? What plans did he have? Why did Haman cry? What eventually happens to a person who wants to destroy others?

3. Psalm 126:5. What does it mean to "sow in tears?" Do people often express deep concern for the lost? How? What feelings do we have for the unsaved?

4. Ecclesiastes 4:1. Why do oppressed people sometimes cry? Why do some people oppress others? In what ways can we help those who are mistreated?

5. Jeremiah 9:1. Why did Jeremiah weep? Why did Israel face stark tragedy? How does the message of Jeremiah 9:18, 13:17, and 14:17 apply to us?

6. Luke 7:38, 44. What did the "sinful woman" do in the story? What response do we make over our sins? What reaction does Christ have when we repent?

7. Acts 20:19, 31. How did Paul serve Christ? Are you acquainted with some Christians who follow his example? Why should we follow Paul's example?

8. Hebrews 5:7. Do you remember that Jesus sometimes shed tears? When or why did He weep? Do we often become too hard-hearted to weep?

9. Hebrews 12:17. Who was Esau and why did he shed tears? See Genesis 25:25-34 and 27:30-38. Why and when does crying sometimes come too late?

10. Revelation 21:4. Why do people cry? Why will God dry up the tears of His people in heaven? How can we help those who weep?

Temptations

—〰—

Martin Luther said, "You can't keep the birds from flying over your head, but you can keep them from building nests in your hair." Temptations "fly" all around us. However, we do not have to yield to them. Let's look at verses that relate to temptations.

1. Matthew 4:1-11. What do you think about the Spirit leading Jesus into the wilderness to be tempted? What three temptations did Jesus face? How do they apply to us?

2. Matthew 6:13. What do you think of the words of Jesus' prayer, "Lead us not into temptation?" Does God tempt His people? Who does God deliver us from? How?

3. Mark 14:38. When Jesus was in Gethsemane and prayed, what did the disciples do? Why didn't they stay awake? To avoid temptations, what should we do?

4. 1 Corinthians 7:5. This verse deals with the subject of intimate relationships. How can Satan tempt the husband and wife who refrain from God-ordained sex?

5. 1 Corinthians 10:13. Why do you think that temptations are common experiences of everyone? In what areas do temptations strike? What resources do the tempted have?

6. Galatians 6:1. How do you feel about anyone who becomes a victim of temptation whether it be theft, profanity, or something else? Should the fallen be trampled?

7. 1 Thessalonians 3:5. Why does the devil look upon God's people as a prize to be won? Because Satan sometimes wins a victory, should that deter us from our work?

8. Hebrews 2:18. When Jesus faced temptations, how did He suffer? Since Jesus is now our faithful high priest in heaven, how can He help those who are tempted?

9. Hebrews 4:15-16. Since Jesus endured temptations without falling, how does He feel about those who meet temptations today? What resource is ours through Him?

10. James 1:13-14. What does James say about a believer being tempted? What are some causes of temptation? What does James 4:7 say about victory over them?

Think or ponder

—〰—

Most people have ten to fifteen billion brain cells. God made us so that we may think and learn. And yet, we never use one half of our abilities to reason and think through the vital issues that we face. One Frenchman wrote, "I think; therefore I am." Isn't it time for us to think about what we think about?

1. Proverbs 23:7. The Bible says that a person is what he thinks. This verse refers to a greedy man. Be careful with his offers. Do we think seriously about life?

2. Matthew 22:41-46. What do you think of Jesus? Whose Son is He? See His words in John 3:16. What do you say about Christ?

3. Luke 2:19. Shepherds came to see "baby Jesus." Mary thought about the miracle of Jesus for months. What truths do you think she treasured in her heart about Him?

4. John 5:39-40. Jesus told religious leaders who searched the Scriptures that they thought they had eternal life. Why didn't they have everlasting life?

5. Romans 12:3. Many books encourage us to have a greater image of ourselves. What does this Scripture tell us to do? How are we to think about self?

6.   1 Corinthians 10:12. Sometimes various teams think they will defeat their opponents, but they lose. Why? Why does a person who is doing well need to be careful?

7.   Ephesians 3:20. Can God help you in any circumstance of life? What does this verse say God can do? How far-reaching and what is the measure of His help?

8.   Philippians 4:8. Many movies use profanity and immoral scenes. Society is plagued by "garbage." Make a list from this verse of the virtues we should think about.

9.   Hebrews 12:3. We are to think and consider Jesus. What did He face during His earthly ministry? How does His example and presence help the ones who hurt?

10.   1 Peter 4:12. Christians have faced many trials across the centuries. What should we think when "fiery trials" come our way? How do we prepare for them?

Time

—〰—

A sundial is located on the campus of Harvard University. The school's founding fathers placed the following inscription on it: "Upon every minute hangs eternity." They wanted every student to understand the value of time. The Bible mentions time over and over again, challenging all of us to recognize the importance of every moment. Let's explore what the Bible teaches about time.

1. Numbers 20:15-16. Moses reminded the Hebrews that they had been in Egypt for a long time. How long do we stay in "Egypt?" Should we move? Why or why not?

2. 1 Chronicles 12:32. The men of Issachar understood the times and were ready to see David become king. Do we understand our times? How can Jesus be our King?

3. Psalm 41:1. In times of trouble, God wants to deliver those who help others. What kind of troubles do we face? How can we help the Lord deliver others?

4. Psalm 56:3. How can we trust the Lord during fearful times? When do dangerous times come? Who faces fears that God can alleviate? Why do we become fearful?

5. Psalm 119:126. When is it time for God "to work?" How does God respond when people disregard His Word? How can we cooperate with God in His work now?

6. Hosea 10:12. Hosea said the time had come to seek the Lord. What kind of "showers" does God want to give? How can we prepare for His blessings?

7. Acts 3:19. What did Simon Peter mean by stating "times of refreshing?" Why do we need that time? What is needed for spiritual refreshing to take place in our lives?

8. Ephesians 5:16. How can we redeem time? How do we waste time? Why should we redeem time? How can we revolutionize our use of time?

9. Hebrews 5:12. When it is time for Christians to be teachers, what are we doing? Why do most people need others to teach them the basics truths of our faith?

10. 1 Peter 1:17. How do most Christians as well as nonbelievers use their time? How can we spend time being reverent to God, realizing that life is short?

Tongue

—ɷɷ—

A dolph Hitler caused World War II because of his "inflamed tongue." The tongue has also brought encouragement and hope to millions because words of comfort and challenge have been expressed. The tongue is a powerful instrument for good or for evil. Look at what the Bible states about the tongue.

1. Genesis 11:1-2. What did God tell Noah's family to do after the Flood? What did they try to do? How did God intervene? Did God accomplish his original plan?

2. Exodus 4:10. God spoke to Moses about becoming the leader of the Israelites, but Moses said he was not eloquent, and had a stammering tongue. What do we tell God?

3. Psalm 34:12-13. What is one secret of a good life? Do some people speak evil with their tongues? Why do they do this? What's the solution?

4. Psalm 71:24. What was David's plan for his tongue? How long did he say he would praise God for His righteous deeds? What did God do for David and for us?

5. Psalm 137:6. What did David say would happen to his tongue if he forgot Jerusalem? What could take place in our lives if we fail to tell what God does for us?

6. Isaiah 50:4. Why do you think that God gave Isaiah an instructed tongue? What did Isaiah say he would do to help the weary? How can we help others with our words?

7. Isaiah 50:17. Evil weapons are sometimes made to attack God's people. What does God do for His people so that those who accuse them can't be successful?

8. Luke 16:24. The parable of Lazarus and the rich man is well known. What did the rich man ask Abraham to do for him? Why does this parable have meaning today?

9. Acts 2:5-11. During the Pentecost season, people came to Jerusalem from many countries. How were they able to hear the message of Jesus in their own language?

10. James 1:26. If a person says he is religious, but does not control his or her tongue, what two truths are evident in that one's life? Do we have trouble with the tongue?

Trinity

—〜〜—

How do we explain electricity? Most of us would not know how to begin giving a definition of the force called electricity. God in His majesty and greatness remains beyond us. We can be blessed by Him, but to understand and explain God in His manifestations can never be fully done; however we may trust Him.

We recognize that God will always be above and beyond us, not only in our earthly lives, but in eternity as well. Man is limited and finite, but God is infinite. And yet, God reveals Himself as Father, Son, and Holy Spirit.

The Bible never uses the word Trinity. However, the Trinitarian concept appears many times throughout the Bible so that we may understand God a little better. A few examples are Genesis 3:22, Genesis 11:7, and Isaiah 6:8. The "us" suggests a "tri-unity" or three in one — God the Father, Jesus the Son, and the Holy Spirit. Look at a few Scriptures which indicate some ways in which God expresses Himself.

1. Genesis 1:1-2, 26. God's name of "Elohim" which is plural appears here. That name has a singular verb, like "the family is…" Elohim suggests the Trinity.

2. Matthew 3:16-17. Who baptized Jesus? How are the Holy Spirit, Jesus, and the Father involved at that particular time in the life of God's Son?

3.   Matthew 28:19-20. What is this text normally called? What mission did Jesus give His followers? How are they baptized? What promise did Jesus give them?

4.   John 1:3. God brought all things into existence. Who became involved with the Father in the work of creation? Where was Jesus in "the beginning?"

5.   Romans 8:9. The Christian's life is controlled by whom? If the professed believer does not have the Spirit of Christ, what can be said of him?

6.   1 Corinthians 12:3-6. If one is indwelt by the Holy Spirit, what is he or she prepared to say about Jesus by the Spirit of God?

7.   2 Corinthians 13:14. Notice three blessings for a believer. What does the grace of Christ mean? What does God give us? What do we have through the Holy Spirit?

8.   Titus 3:3-6. In what condition does God find some converts? How is the Trinity involved in saving us? What challenges and blessings come to us?

9.   Hebrews 9:13-15. Christ sacrificed His sinless life to God. What two results come to us from His death? What does the new covenant mean?

10.   Jude 1:1, 20-21. God calls and loves His people. What does Christ do for us? As we pray, how are we spiritually built up?

Voices

—◁∞▷—

J oan of Arc, French saint and national heroine (1412-1431), heard "voices" speaking to her, even before her teenage years. She was tried as a heretic and burned at the stake in Rouen, France, on May 30, 1431. When religious authorities asked why she did what she was doing, Joan of Arc said "voices" spoke to her. When church leaders asked why they did not hear the voices, Joan told them that they were not listening.

We need to listen to God's voice. He speaks through creation, His Word, and by the Holy Spirit. We should be deaf to the voice of the world and the devil, but alert to God's voice. Let's go to the Scripture again as we look at the topic of voices.

1. Genesis 22:1-18. What did God ask Abraham to do? What did an angel say to Abraham? Because of his obedience, what promise did God give Abraham?

2. Exodus 5:1-2. When Moses and Aaron visited Pharaoh, what did they say to him? What answer did Pharaoh give? Why do people still question God?

3. 1 Kings 19:1-18. Why did Elijah go to Mt. Horeb? What did God's voice ask Elijah? What commission did he receive? Does God still have fresh orders for His people?

4. Isaiah 6:1-4. What vision did Isaiah have when Israel's king died? What did that show? What did the angelic beings say? How do we hear God's messages today?

5. Job 4:12-17. In the midst of Job's suffering, describe more of his surroundings. What two questions does this text ask? What do you think of the questions?

6. Isaiah 40:3. Who was the person whose voice would later be heard in the desert? (Matthew 3:3). What was the message? What message do we have to give today?

7. Jeremiah 3:11-15. What did God's voice say to faithless Israel? If they heard and responded, what blessing would they receive? What if we hear or don't hear?

8. Ezekiel 33:30-32. What did the Israelites in Babylon say about Ezekiel's preaching? How did they respond? How do people often respond to God's message today?

9. Revelation 3:20. Who knocks at the door of every life? If people hear Christ speaking and let Him come in, how are their lives blessed?

10. Revelation 11:15. What did the voices in heaven say when the seventh angel blew his trumpet? What will happen to the kingdoms of this world when Jesus returns?

Walk or behavior

—ᴍ—

Most parents remember when their first or fourth child took his or her first step. When a one year old begins to amble across the floor, that one feels excitement throughout his nervous system.

The Bible often mentions the spiritual walk of God's people as well as the evil walk of those who do not belong to the Lord. When a person is walking with the Lord, he or she can be useful in God's cause.

1. Genesis 5:24. Because of Enoch's righteous life just before the Flood, God translated Enoch to heaven. How can we walk with God in the time of evil and wickedness?

2. Genesis 17:1-2. What did God ask Abraham to do? What did the Lord promise him? Is the Christian life easy? What will God do for those who live right today?

3. Leviticus 26:3-13. What promises did God give Israel if they would live right? What special promise is found in verse 12? Why could they and we believe God?

4. Psalm 1:1. When does God say He will bless His people? What abstentions did God call for? Why is it necessary today to refrain from the evil practices of the world?

5. Psalm 23:4. When God is our Shepherd, how can we face death? Why don't we have to be afraid? What kind of life does God give us? Then what happens?

6. Psalm 84:11. Memorize this verse. What does God become for His people? What does this mean? What promise does the Lord give to those who live uprightly?

7. Amos 3:3. If two people do not have the same convictions, what could happen to them? What can bring people together so they may live in harmony?

8. Galatians 5:16-18. What does it mean to walk in the Holy Spirit or be led by the Spirit? What victory does a spiritual walk give a person? Is this difficult?

9. 1 John 1:7. What does it mean to walk in the light? Who is with us in the light? What two great advantages does this kind of walk give a person?

10. 2 John 1:2. Why did John feel full of joy as he wrote this brief letter? What does it mean to walk in truth? Why should we be truthful? Who commands this? Why?

War

—ᘑ—

The world has been plagued with war since the beginning of time. When we read history books, a greater part of those events relate to wars. Battles go on in every country. We also have spiritual wars that go on within the souls of men. Let's look at warfare scenes.

1. 1 Chronicles 5:18-22. A war began between the descendants of Hagar and Sarah. Why was prayer important? What did the Hagarites lose? Who claims the victory?

2. Psalm 55:21; 120:7. What are the words of a person like who wants to go to war? What is man's problem? When the "olive branch" is extended, what happens?

3. Eccclesiastes 9:18. Why is wisdom better than weapons of war? What might be the solution of a lot of today's wars? Do nations seek God's wisdom in relationships?

4. Isaiah 2:4; Micah 4:3. If we let God have His way in our lives, what would He teach us? What do the two Scriptures by God's prophets teach us about a warless world?

5. Isaiah 41:11-13. What will take place in the lives of those who war against God's people? What does God promise His people? What's the lesson for today?

6. Luke 14:31. What does a wise king do before he leads his forces into battle? What does Jesus teach us about our following Him into spiritual warfare?

7. Luke 21:7. Until Christ returns, what is going to continue in the world? Why will a big change not take place? What's the hope for nations who fight and war?

8. 2 Corinthians 10:3-5. How is spiritual war different from the world's battles? What kinds of weapons do Christians have? Do we use our weapons? What do they do?

9. James 4:1-2. What did James say causes warfare among God's people? Why don't we get what we want? Where does warfare start? How do we pray in the wrong way?

10. 1 Peter 2:11. What definition is given to God's people who live in this world? What are a few sinful desires that we face? How do fleshly lusts war against the soul?

Water

—∿∿—

Some of South America's impressive sights include the waterfalls of Iguazu. Those falls on the border between Brazil, Paraguay, and Argentina attract thousands of visitors every year. Water gets the attention of the youngest child to the oldest adult.

Water is made up of two parts of hydrogen to one part of oxygen. Without water, life would end for plants and animals. We recognize the blessing or blight that comes from water-laden clouds. Samuel Taylor Coleridge painted a glowing description of water in "The Rime of the Ancient Mariner." He wrote, "Water, water every where, And all the boards did shrink; Water, water, every where, and not a drop to drink....Day after day, day after day, We stuck, nor breath nor motion ; As idle as a painted ship Upon a painted ocean.. Let's see a few lines about water from the Bible's perspective.

1.   Genesis 1:2, 20. How did water become a part of creation? How did God's Spirit involve water? What command did God give to the inhabitants of the oceans?

2.   Exodus 14:26. When God liberated the Israelites from Egypt, what did the forces of Pharaoh do? What happened to them? How did the Israelites fare?

3.   2 Kings 2:21. What did Elisha discover near Jericho? How did he help? What did the salt represent? How can God make a difference where we live?

4. Psalm 42:1. What happens to deer when they become thirsty? Do people have a spiritual thirst today? What does this mean? How is God able to help?

5. Isaiah 43:2. What does it mean that people pass through "deep waters?" How do those who face tough times survive? How does God use us to help?

6. Isaiah 44:3-4. What does it mean to have water poured upon the thirsty land physically and spiritually? What's it like to live near God's "flowing streams?"

7. Isaiah 58:10-11. Where may the hungry and oppressed be found? What is our duty to such people? What happens to those who give help to the needy?

8. Jeremiah 2:13. Describe a cistern. What is a "broken cistern?" What value is a broken tank or reservoir. When people forsake God, what do they have?

9. John 7:37-39. What invitation does Jesus give to those who have a spiritual thirst? What happens to those who receive Jesus? What flows from a believer's life?

10. Corinthians 3:6. In God's kingdom, what two kinds of workers are vital? Who brings about the increase? Can we take credit for the increase? Why or why not?

Wicked

—⟪⟫—

Many people know something about wicked rulers from the time of Nero to Hitler. A wicked person is one who does evil or wrong. The prophet Ezekiel used the word wicked about 40 times to describe some of the people of God in his day.

Wickedness continues all over the world today. Let's see what the Bible says about wicked empires or people.

1. Genesis 6:5. How do you think God sees the wickedness of the world? How does He feel about it? In the midst of evil men, who does God always see?

2. Genesis 13:12-13. Who chose to live in Sodom? Why? If you had a choice like Lot did, what would you do? How do people express themselves against God?

3. Genesis 39:5-10. What kind of a person was Joseph? Who tried to entice him to do wrong? What response did Joseph make? What would be your reaction?

4. 1 Samuel 24:17. Do the wicked expect to be silenced? Why or why not? What happens to them? How does God become involved with the wicked?

5. 2 Chronicles 7:14. Who first received the message of this text? When did God promise to bless His people? If we receive God's blessings, what must we do?

6. Psalm 37:35-38. Do the wicked sometimes flourish? Do you ever become jealous or envious of their seeming success? What's the future of the wicked?

7. Proverbs 11:5, 21, 31. What hope do the wicked have? Do you think they give serious consideration to punishment that awaits them? What's their reward?

8. Isaiah 55:7. What can or should the wicked do to have their lives saved? What will God do for those who are on the wrong path when they turn back to Him?

9. Matthew 13:38. In the Parable of the Tares or weeds, who sowed the evil seed? How did he do it? What happens at the end of the age to the evil ones?

10. Romans 1:26-32. Do you think the people in Paul's day lived as wickedly as people do today? In what ways did they live? What hope do wicked people have?

Wine

—ɯɯ—

S ome reports state that about one-half of the fatal accidents on the highways come about as a result of drinking or drunk drivers. The cost in car insurance goes up continually, and one reason relates to wine. A large percentage of health problems world-wide evolve because of abuses in using alcoholic beverages. The Bible gives many insights into the use of alcohol, some positive, but mostly negative. Let's see what we can learn about alcohol from the Bible.

1. Genesis 9:20-21. After the Flood, what did Noah do? What disgrace happened to him and his family? Will a "binge of drinking" still have evil effects?

2. Genesis 19:30-36. After the destruction of Sodom, what did Lot's two daughters do? What two nations came about because of that incest? Why is drinking dangerous?

3. Proverbs 20:1; 23:29-30. How does wine mock a person? What critical problems often take place with those who drink? Why is it best not to drink?

4. Isaiah 5:11-15. How do people abuse the use of wine? What takes place in the lives of those who become addicted to drink?

5. Daniel 1:8, 15-16. When Daniel was in Babylon, what did he and his friends refuse to do? What happened with their health? Why is it more healthy not to drink?

6. Matthew 11:19. John the Baptist didn't indulge in celebrations, but what did people say of him. What did some say of Jesus? What will some critics always do?

7. John 2:1-11. When Jesus attended a wedding, what did His mother say to Him? What did Jesus do? Are celebrations always wrong? What did the disciples do?

8. Ephesians 5:18. Does this Scripture prove total abstinence? What does over-indulgence lead to? Why is it best for Christians to be filled with the Spirit?

9. 1 Timothy 5:23. Why did Paul tell Timothy to take a little wine for his stomach's sake? Does medicine contain alcohol? What does this teach us?

10. 1 Peter 4:3-5. Many believers in New Testament times had what kind of a previous lifestyle? When Christians change, what do former friends sometimes say?

Wisdom

—⟋⟍—

Socrates was a man of Athens, Greece. He was born nearly four hundred years before Christ. The world continues to speak about the wisdom of Socrates. Would we like to live and be remembered as wise people? The Bible points out the route of wisdom for all who will follow it. Let's explore this topic of wisdom that gave much pride to the ancient Grecians as well as people in our day.

1. Job 28:28. According to Job, what is the beginning of wisdom? Do many people fear the Lord today? Why or why not? How does the fear of God keep us from evil?

2. Psalm 104:24. When we contemplate the thousands wonders of creation, how do we think it all came about? Has man ever made a universe? How did God do it?

3. Proverbs 4:7. What is the principal need in life? How do we get wisdom? Is this a self-accomplishment? How does wisdom demonstrate itself in life?

4. Matthew 7:24. Why is a house on a "rock" better than a house on the "sand?" What happens to both when storms come? What is the message for our lives?

5. Matthew 13:54. When Jesus returned to Nazareth where He grew up, what did the people say of Him? Where did Christ get His wisdom? What about us?

6. Luke 2:40. When Jesus was twelve years of age, how was He described? What areas of growth did Jesus experience? How does His growth fit into our life style?

7. Romans 11:33. What kind of depths of wisdom and knowledge are in God? What does it mean that God's ways are past finding out? How do we feel about it?

8. Colossians 2:3. What does Scripture mean when it states that all the treasures of wisdom are in Christ? How does He know about the past, present, and future?

9. James 1:5. Do we feel that we need wisdom? Why? If God is the source of wisdom how do we get it? What is God's reaction when we make requests of Him?

10. James 3:17. Where may God's wisdom be found? How may we describe God's wisdom? Is God's wisdom demonstrated in our lives? Why or why not?

Wives

—∿—

A legendary story about Adam fascinates some people. He said to the Lord one day, "God, I love life here in the garden, but I sometimes feel lonesome. Can you give me someone to be with me?" When the Lord asked man what he wanted, Adam began to describe his wishes. Then God said, "Adam what you are telling me might cost you an arm and a leg." Adam said, "Lord, what would you give me for a rib?" What can be said about a wife?

1. Genesis 2:18-25. Why did God give Adam a wife? How did God provide a "help meet" for the first man? What do you think Adam said when he saw Eve?

2. Genesis 3:4, 20. How, when, and where did the devil become involved in Eve's life? Who gave Eve her name? What does the name mean?

3. Genesis 24:1-4. Where did Abraham send his servant to get a wife for his son? Why didn't Isaac marry someone where he lived? (See Genesis 28:1-5).

4. Job 2:9-10. What counsel did Job's wife give him? Why? What did Job say to her? What do we say to one another during tough times?

5. Proverbs 18:22. Finding a wife has what quality? What blessing comes from God when a man marries? What favors would you like to have in your marriage?

6. Ezekiel 24:18. Who was Ezekiel and where did he live most of his life? What did he think of his wife? What happened to her? What should a man feel about his wife?

7. Malachi 2:13-16. Why did God tell men that their worship was not acceptable? How does God feel about divorce? Does God forgive us when family life fails?

8. Matthew 22:18. Read this amazing story. What does Jesus say about marriage in heaven? What will be the composition of family life in heaven?

9. Titus 2:4-5. How should the wife relate to her husband? Discuss 1 Corinthians 7:3-5, 10-16 and Ephesians 5:21-22. What does "submission to one another" mean?

10. 1 Peter 3:4-5. What did Simon Peter write about the wife's true beauty? What can husbands do to enhance the beauty of their wives?

Work or labor

—ɯ—

A man shared a testimony in church one night, saying, *I want all of you to know that I have been on God's train to glory for 47 years.* Someone who knew him quite well whispered to a neighbor, *Yeah, and old Jim ain't done much more than wear out the brakes all along the way!*

Whether we are on a farm, working as secretaries or teachers, keeping the house, or climbing telephone poles, everyone knows that we have the responsibility of work. The Bible challenges us to do something for the betterment of the world and for His glory. Look at a few Scriptures that challenge us in the area of work.

1. Genesis 2:15. God created Adam and placed him in the Garden of Eden, telling him he had a job to do. We still have work to do. How is work is a blessing?.

2. Nehemiah 4:4-6, 21. The Hebrews returned from captivity in Babylon. They rebuilt the walls of their city. Verse 21 states that they continued working. Should we?

3. Proverbs 24:30-34. Those who don't work have thorns, not crops. Those who sleep all the time come to poverty. What ills of society may be solved by work?

4. Matthew 5:16. Jesus says our lights should shine so that others may see our "good works" and glorify God. How is God glorified by what we do?

5. John 9:3-4. No person has ever worked more than Jesus. He said God is busy. When does our work come to a close? Name some works of Jesus.

6. 1 Corinthians 3:9. Have you ever thought of being God's partner in the work you do? What did Paul say about work? We work "with" God. Discuss this.

7. 1 Corinthians 15:58. Since a great future awaits God's people, what are some ways we need to work? What did Paul say about work in God's kingdom?

8. Ephesians 2:8-10. How do we become Christians. If God's grace saves us, why should we work? What kind of work should we do? What does Paul call us?

9. 2 Thessalonians 3:10-13. What does Paul say about those who refuse to work? Would many die of starvation today if they didn't work? What about verse 13?

10. Hebrews 10:24. How do we encourage others to work? How do we teach children and young people to work? What are some good deeds that everyone can do?

Worship

—〰—

True spiritual worship is the recognition and reverence of God as the Lord of all. One of the Psalms states that the heavens declare God's glory and His handiwork. We bow before God, we esteem Him, we lift up His glorious name individually and as a congregation. In our praying, singing, and daily work, we should continually worship the Lord. The Bible encourages our worship. Let's consider this subject.

1. Exodus 23:25. God said that if we worship Him that He would send His blessings upon what life-sustaining needs? What other blessing comes from worship?

2. Deuteronomy 26:5-13. The Hebrews took their "first fruits" unto God. He brought Israel from Egypt to Palestine. They worshiped through offerings. Should we?

3. Job 1:20. What did Job do after he lost his earthly blessings? Is there a *wrong* time to worship? What "worship attitude" is ours in good as well as in horrible times?

4. Ezekiel 8:14, 16 The Hebrews worshiped Tamuz, nature's god. They gave cakes to the pagan *Queen of Heaven*. (Jeremiah 7:18; 44:17-19, 25). Why was that wrong?

5. Matthew 2:10-11. Wise men from the east journeyed to Bethlehem, giving gifts to Jesus and they worshiped Him. Do we worship Jesus? (Philippians 2:5-11).

6. Matthew 14:28-33. When the disciples encountered a storm, Jesus rescued them. What did they say about Christ and what did they do?

7. Matthew 28:17; Luke 24:52. When the disciples met Jesus just before His ascension, what did they do? What reaction did they have? What's our reaction to worship?

8. John 4:24. Jesus met a particular woman of Samaria at Jacob's well. What did Jesus teach about the place of worship? What two vital elements are in worship?

9. Colossians 2:18. Paul warned against the worship of angels. Does Romans 1:25 exclude worship of all creation? Who only is to be worshiped?

10. Revelation 5:13-14. This picture in heaven includes the angels worshiping God and His Son. What other group is seen in worship? How do we worship?

Postlude

—〜〜—

When John Wesley was reading the preface of Martin Luther's commentary on Romans, he said that he felt his heart *strangely warmed*. As you read the Scriptures and discuss the questions in this book, your heart may be *strangely warmed*.

This book can be used by any group or individual. Tell your friends about this topical work to everyone who wants to delve more deeply into the *Book of the ages*. The words of one poet speak clearly: "God's Word is like a deep, deep mine; and jewels rich and rare, are hidden in its mighty depths, for every searcher there." One need in the lives of many people is to become "addicted" to God's Word. For the Lord's glory, share with others this Scripture-saturated book, will you?

The price of the book is $13.95 from Xulon, and they give a **30% discount** to pastors and churches.

You may order the book **online** by typing *Xulon Press com* in the white bar on your computer (as you know), going to their bookstore link, then typing in the book title or author's name. The book is available through Barnes and Noble, Target, Amazon.com, Borders, and religious bookstores.

Please note also: Tate Publishing has published Taylor's books on *The 13 Apostles* (228 pp.) and *Jesus: King of Kings* (Revelation, 296 pp.). These books are easy to read, sound in teaching, and highly inspirational. Call Tate Publishing toll-free at 1-888-361-9473 or order through Barnes and Noble or religious bookstores. Rich blessings to you as you let the Bible become the most important book in your life.

What some are saying about the *102 Fascinating Bible Topics for Group Discussions*

—ᨶᨵᨷ—

My friend, former classmate, and colleague, Preston Taylor has composed a delightful topical study of the Bible for small groups. His presentation is easy for any person to use and share in an intimate setting….a superb piece of work through research of the Scriptures. This book will "keep you in the Bible."
— Billy D. Dunn, BA, BD, M.Ed, D.Min. etc.
Colonel USAR (Ret.); Director Chaplaincy services,
Lufkin State School, Texas.

Preston Taylor presents an excellent theme study for small groups. The ten thought-provoking questions on each of the 102 chapters inspire the group members to make a thorough Scripture study — relating those findings to the daily Christian walk.
— Dave (B.S. Glenville State University, Glenville, West Virginia) and Jane Posey, Owners of Dane Trucking Company, Houston (Tomball) Texas.

The Bible topics in this writing are wide ranging, the Scriptures apt, and the questions are simple enough for a beginner, yet provocative enough to challenge a life-long scholar.
— Betty Hicks Clay. Graduate of Ouachita Baptist University and Southwestern Baptist Seminary. As a retired mathematics teacher, Betty writes magazine articles about genealogy and computer technology.

What a wonderful, innovative idea Preston Taylor has given us in this Book! A group or an individual may go in many directions with these studies, and you are going to be blessed no matter which approach you choose. The word will not return void; the power is always there!

— Mike Stone. Retired teacher, B.A., M.A. Pastor, FBC, Crystal City, Texas

This book of "102 Bible themes" is a unique and exciting way of allowing God to speak to us "one word at a time." It lends itself to both individual and group study.

— Beth Church. Retired school teacher who continues to be totally involved in God's kingdom cause across the decades.

The "102 Bible Topics" present a practical and wise approach for group discussions. The journey through this book will enhance each person's spiritual growth and cause each one to know how to handle God's Word in a better way.

— Raul Hernandez. Vietnam helicopter pilot. South Texas pastor, and retired school teacher and principal.

Printed in the United States
49895LVS00004B/1-132

9 781600 341311